#REMOTE WORKING!

25 highly experienced professionals share their very best advice for remote working and working effectively in challenging times.

WRITING MATTERS

#RemoteWorking

First published in April 2020

Writing Matters Publishing (UK)
info@writingmatterspublishing.com
www.writingmatterspublishing.com

ISBN 978-1-912774-49-4 (e-book)
ISBN 979-8-632733-13-7 (pbk)

Editor: Andrew Priestley

Contributors: Penny Power OBE, Kim-Adele Platts, Ben Phillips, Janelle Mansfield, Ian Hale, Michelle Harris, James Barrington-Brown, Susan Popoola, Robert Hayward, Safa Arif, Adesola Orimalade, Jo Baldwin Trott, Nick Meinertshagen, Mike Davis-Marks OBE, Megan Germann, David Rothwell, Padma Coram, Marc Karschies, Dympna Kennedy, Kalpesh Patel, Marcia Brown, Luke Murfitt, Su Patel, Phil Lewis, Ben Phillips and Andrew Priestley.

A CIP catalogue record for this book is available from the British Library.

Contents

Embrace Change

Foreword Penny Power OBE

Twenty-two years ago, I became a remote worker. With three children under five, I decided to take control of my time, space and life and manage the two things that mattered most to me: my family and my career, my way.

I guess you could say that alongside my decision to marry and to become a mum, this ranks in the top three decisions in my life that I had control over. All three are life changing and their success is directly proportional to the effort, love and self-development that you choose to put in.

Additionally, they are proportional to the selfless acts you make, your ability to care for others and manage the ups and downs.

I want to share what I mean by *have control of*; do we control when we fall in love? Do we control when we become a parent? Do we control when the need to work remotely comes into our life? Not always. We can, however, control how we react to these things. In anger, in fear or in trust and faith and with the true understanding of our deepest values and desires to make the most of our lives, whatever it presents.

What is very clear to me, and easier said in hindsight, is that your life can be as beautiful and empowering as you make it. I have chosen to embrace change, to empower myself and others to cope with it and to be the best that I can be despite adversity, trauma, fear and uncertainty that I have faced.

These words come to mind regularly, they were from my dear mum, when I was in my early 20s: "Darling, never drop your standards to those of others".

It made me consider what my 'standards' and own personal values were. Who did I want to be? I focus on this at all times, I do not worry about *what* I am.

Our life is full of changes; our *what* can be expressed by labels we give ourselves *I am a mother, I am a wife, I am a business women, I am self-employed, I am unemployed.* In life, our *what* will change, sometimes dramatically, and without us having any control over it. What doesn't have to change is our *who.*

Who you are deep inside will determine the road you take when you face change. Throughout this beautifully and passionately created book, I want you to embrace the way each writer has loved you, their commitment to give you the skills and the mindset to manage change and perhaps to manage overwhelm. Remember, when you take deep breaths, when you create your list of thoughts from reading, this is your journey in life, your choices and you are in control of who you are and what you become as a result of your new awakenings.

With love to you and with the empathy of knowing, sometimes, we have to dig very deep to find our own path to happiness.

Penny Power OBE

... And Then Suddenly The World Changed ...

Andrew Priestley Editor

In February 2020, I was on a plane to Australia and at 2am I disembarked at Abu Dhabi airport and everyone was wearing face masks. When I arrived eight hours later at Melbourne Airport Australia, a normally busy airport was almost empty. The connecting bus that is usually full was empty. I had heard about the virus, discounted it and thought of it like any other winter flu.

Just so you know, at the time of writing - March 2020 - the Coronavirus 19 (COVID-19) was officially declared a worldwide pandemic by the World Health Organisation (WHO). And today, like most of the world, the UK is in lock-down - for 21 days, maybe more. And we are required to self isolate, stay at home unless it is essential travel i.e., food shopping, medical, emergencies. The roads are conspicuously and eerily empty.

Suddenly we are social distancing. We are advised to keep at least two metres away from friends and family.

Essentially, nearly everything is shut. We probably knew it was serious when McDonalds closed their doors.

Some people still think this is a joke. There's a certain unreality about it. As I write, the number of people who died in the UK from advanced COVID-19 complications doubled in 24 hours and the NHS reluctantly reported that they only had capacity to treat one in seven patients with severe symptoms with doctors imploring Brits to stay at home. Their number one concern is the NHS's ability to cope. The coronavirus attacks the lungs like a virulent pneumonia. The treatment is to put people on respirators and the NHS simply doesn't have enough.

The critical recommendation: stay at home.

My grandmother experienced The Spanish Flu pandemic. It lasted from January 1918 to December1920, infected over 500 million people. The death toll is estimated between 17 and 50 million. One hundred years later, world is vastly different. We have instant communication, in most cases, governments cooperating and responding rapidly and medical resources that were not available to my grandmother's generation. And we can already see the positive effects of social distancing in the peaking and tapering off of Covid cases and deaths.

In late March, it is Spring. We have come through a cold winter and the sun is out. Despite the Government imploring people to self isolate we saw masses of people out in force. On the second last Monday of March the Government imposed State Emergency laws that require you to stay home.

And this means work from home.

For some people this is a strange and unfamiliar situation. Foreign even. The routine is totally disrupted. There is no commute. No ID entry. No early morning chats. And right now, there's no choice. Work from home. Make it work. Carry on. And for many that is a steep learning curve.

For others, the authors in this book, they have been working remotely for years either as entrepreneur or self-employed within the gig economy. For them, it is business as usual. They have mastered the commute from the bedroom via the kitchen to the home office. They have figured out what works and what doesn't.

They have learned how to juggle family responsibilities with client demands. Most professional women are wondering what the fuss is all about because they have balanced family and work commitments for ever.

Some of our authors have not only worked from home but have been running remote teams for years. Again they have figured out what works.

They understand the technology. A daily huddle on Zoom or Skype or whatever and connect as needed throughout the day. Work gets done via Google docs, DropBox ... Trello ... again whatever software suits their needs.

But they also monitor remote performance differently, too.

Most or our authors are a) providing professional services, b) remote working and/or b) running remote teams. And doing it profitably. Many have even scaled this configuration.

All the articles in #Remote Working relate to this context.

In some cases, they are describing best practice. In others cases, they are sharing how they have adapted or pivoted to cope with the current circumstances.

In any case, the world will be very different once this crisis passes. We have learned that we can adapt, adjust and innovate. We have discovered we can streamline and work just as efficiently. Companies are already planning to trim excesses now that they know the world can work remotely.

That in itself is the next big challenge.

I am proud to edit a book that gives you extensive wisdom, solid practical advice across a broad spectrum of issues, smart cuts and generous encouragement to master remote working.

This is THE book for our current times. Stay calm. Enjoy.

The Virtual Water Cooler

Making Remote Working Work For You Including My Top 5 Tips For Leading A Remote Team.

Kim Adele

As the coronavirus continues to spread, and the talk of social distancing is gaining momentum, many people are facing the prospect of working remotely.

As a remote worker already, I understand the benefits it brings, including flexibility and the time you get back from removing the commute.

That said it does have it's downside with many people feeling more isolated as they miss the connections. The loss of the water cooler conversations can have a devastating impact on how connected we feel.

When I first became a remote worker, I hadn't realised the impact this would have on me, and how much I missed the daily interaction with people.

It can be hard to get used to the move to remote working and to keep the boundaries of working and not working. If you aren't careful you can start to feel like you never switch off.

It is essential to build your boundaries. I have a set working day, and just like going into an actual office I get ready for work and go to my office (or workspace if you don't have a separate room) with everything I need for the day. I have a kettle and drinks there to enable me to treat it like a real office and not get distracted by things in my normal life. I have also learnt that you can so quickly get distracted when you are in an actual office, people can see that you are busy and in meetings.

In contrast, when you work from home, you have to be mindful that we carry a misconception that *working from home* might be perceived as *shirking from home.*

We know this is not true, but if it is in our subconscious, it will drive us to make the wrong decisions.

We know we are busy working, either in meetings or completing our work and yet our desire to prove your productivity can have us immediately answering emails and calls the second they come in. We also will check social media thinking it will just take a minute, and yet we know it will take longer really. Working like this is not productive; it has been shown that a distraction, such as answering an email, can have a 20-minute impact on our flow. I now schedule time to read my emails and to check social media, I read them first thing, at lunch and again at the end of the day, enabling me to concentrate on my meetings and the work I need to do. When I have an essential piece of work, I put my phone on do not disturb and turn notifications off on my laptop to enable me to get in the flow and be my most productive. The last thing I do in each day is writing my to-do list for tomorrow; this enables me to be confident there is nothing critical outstanding and allows me to switch off from work. If in writing this I identify something significant that needs my attention immediately I will work overtime in the same way you would in a traditional office, the benefit of this is you are making a conscious decision, and you recognise it. I do still occasionally check my emails on my phone once I have finished work for the day, although I have always done this, so it is less about working remotely and more about my working style.

Another challenge I faced was leading a peripatetic team, as I found my colleagues also struggled with the perceived disconnection that can result from working remotely.

As their leader, I realised I needed to find a way to motivate and engage my team and that I would need to find some innovative ways to do so. I started to investigate the ways to reconnect and enable us to work collaboratively from our remote environments.

Fortunately, the speed with which technology is evolving means there are now several apps, pieces of software you can use which enable to address this disconnect.

My Top Tips For Leading A Remote Team

- **Keep communicating** - WhatsApp groups are great for this as they are quick to set up and allow for you to dedicate groups for specific reasons. I usually have groups set up for particular pieces of work which enable all those working on them to collaborate. It is also worth setting up a group 'water cooler' to allow colleagues to engage in less formal and more personal level.
- **Stay visible** - Use Video Calls; whether for team meetings or for 121 calls as this allows you to see if anyone in your team is looking disconnected and might need more support. I use Zoom or Skype - these are a great way to run video conference calls either with an individual or with a group. You can share screens enabling you to work through documents, and you can record them to allow people to revisit and replay. As human beings we are social creatures and we need to be connected. Keeping a visual connection allows you to identify anyone who is feeling the isolation.
- **Collaboration** - ensure there is a way for your team to continue to collaborate. There are some simple applications such as Trello, MS Teams, which enable you to keep track of your work and also to create team boards and share work. Uploading tasks and documents to allow colleagues to work collaboratively on them. Plan your time - use a shared

calendar so people can see when you are free if they need to have a call with you. Also be conscious of your boundaries, just because you are working from home does not mean you should be available 24/7 you do need to have time to recharge for your mental wellbeing.

- **Schedule 121s** - just because you are working remotely doesn't take away the importance of valuable time with your team on an individual basis to understand what is going well, what they are working on and what support they need from you. Also, to ensure they are still getting personal development. Which can easily get forgotten for remote workers, who become unsure of the options available to them. As their leader, you can guide them through this.
- **Feedback** - don't fall into the out of sight out of mind trap. When we work in person, we thank people for a job well done, recognise their success in front of colleagues. Failing to do this can be a cause for disengagement as remote workers can feel very task-driven without this invaluable recognition of their part in the team.

I found doing these enabled me to maintain a highly motivated remote team with a shared sense of purpose. We did sometimes augment this with a virtual social gathering such as a virtual quiz to allow us also to connect less formally.

Leading a remote team can be tricky, however, following the same disciplines you do in face to face management and tailoring them to the virtual world with the augmentation of technology will allow you to do this successfully.

Being a remote worker and/or a remote leader has its challenges, but it also has enormous benefits, you get your commute time back, and you can choose how you use it. I had often struggled to work on my self-development or my fitness. I now get up at the same time I used to and use the time I would be commuting to instead alternate exercise or self-study.

It has enabled me to have more balance in my life and has accelerated my career.

About Kim-Adele Platts

Kim-Adele Platts FInstLM is an Interim CEO, entrepreneur and board-level coach who specialises in helping executives lead with impact and humanity. Her journey has taken her from an NVQ in hairdressing to the boardrooms of the FTSE 250.

With over 25 years of experience, Kim has established a reputation as a transformational leader. She consistently generates new business and has turned underperforming companies into market leaders despite challenging environments.

She speaks internationally on business and is a Non-Exec Director with the IoD, Academy Trust and Mary's Meals.

www.kimadele.org

https://twitter.com/kimadele10

https://www.linkedin.com/in/kimadele/

https://www.facebook.com/kimadele10/

https://www.youtube.com/channel

https://www.instagram.com/stories/kimadele10/?hl=en

Getting Immersive While Being Remote - For Long-Term Business Success

Janelle Mansfield

As we navigate the new world order that is working remotely, or working from home, I encourage you all to consider this as an opportunity. Let me explain.

For seven years I was in a role that required me to either work remotely, or to travel a significant amount of time. Often the travel was only necessitated by a lack of willingness by my company or my colleagues to embrace collaborative technologies. This caused the business to incur unnecessary costs and required me to spend a lot of unproductive time travelling. More than that, it was a drain on my physical and emotional well-being and my travel schedule became the critical path. For me, practically speaking, participating remotely was rarely an option as I couldn't fully follow important conversations, or contribute in a meaningful way.

Now, fast forward to early 2021.

Let's imagine we *#flattenthecurve* and are able to resume normal business operations. Will we embrace the new remote collaboration skills we've all learned, and I expect mastered, during the COVID-19 pandemic or will we happily retreat and go back to our old, costly ways of doing business?

I argue that this forced remote working situation in an opportunity. And a large one at that. We can now take the time to test out different collaboration tools, establish best practices, and get comfortable with engaging with our colleagues, stakeholders and customers in a much more flexible way.

Why Working Remotely Presents A Business Opportunity

People: It better accommodates for different participation and personality styles (think extrovert vs. introvert) and provides more flexibility for different learning styles (visual, auditory, kinesthetic). This creates more engagement and higher quality participation.

Costs: Let's consider the financial cost of requiring individuals to travel either for regular work duties, occasional in-person meetings/workshops/training or the missed opportunity cost of not having key stakeholders involved in an active and productive manner. For businesses this can represent a significant cost.

Employee recruitment: If businesses were more comfortable with remote working scenarios and better set-up to leverage the opportunity this presents, then employee recruitment could be taken to a new level, with borders, distance or geography becoming less of a constraint. This could be especially beneficial for smaller markets, or businesses that want to recruit global talent due to lower salary costs or skills shortages.

Time: Speed can be accelerated by using collaborative technologies for meetings/training/workshops which can be scheduled and delivered without having to consider travel schedules. Additionally, session time can be reduced as you'll no longer be trying to squeeze as much as possible into any given session to *make the best* of Joe or Jane having traveled in.

Customer engagement: As businesses become more comfortable with these technologies, so too will their customers. This creates new opportunities for how, when and the frequency of creating meaningful connection points with customers. How many of us would love to see the face of the employee we are communicating with or show them a video of exactly why a product isn't working.

Practical Steps To Create An Immersive, Yet Remote-Based Collaboration Practice In Your Business

After many years of trial and error, frustration and wasted time and energy, I've come up with this list of practical advice to help you master the art of remote collaboration.

Leverage multiple technology solutions: Consider the use of both a voice/video solution alongside a collaboration tool.

For example, I like to combine Zoom with the use of Mural to replace in person whiteboarding workshops or training.

By leveraging multiple tools simultaneously, participants will be more engaged. They can elect to actively participate in the way that makes the most sense for them.

For myself, an extroverted participant, I like to be able to watch the reactions of my colleagues via video and to verbally share my thoughts when I'm confident in my ideas. If I'm not sure what I'm thinking is a good idea, I like being able to share it in written format, either via chat or through a sticky on Mural.

Simultaneous use of Zoom and Mural for a completely immersive, yet remote, workshop experience.

Provide your teams with access to multiple options, but not too many: Carrying on the idea from above, different meetings will require different tools. Encourage your team to have multiple tool options, but no more than 4 – 5, that they can leverage to best suit their needs i.e., A voice/video tool, a collaboration tool, a document repository with real-time collaboration, a chat tool. Encourage the business to adopt a set of tools, with subscriptions for your teams.

Establish best practices: Once you've decided on which toolset you want to leverage, establish a set of best practices that become standard for each meeting i.e., No overtalking, raising hand to share, use of an agenda, video on/off, round-table, active participation, accommodation for pets/kids/bio breaks, multi-tasking, turning off all notifications, etc.

Lead by example: As a leader, I strongly advise that you model the behaviors you wish your employees and colleagues to display while working remotely. They will take their cue from the leaders and model the behaviors they see demonstrated.

Consider the duration and frequency of meetings: It takes focus and discipline to stay engaged and active in a meeting of any type – regardless of whether or not it is in-person or online. Consider that most people tune out every 15 – 20 minutes and require extended breaks every 90 minutes.

Make it fun, be creative: It's easy for us to get focused on getting through an agenda or specific topic. Allow for up to five minutes of fun at each meeting. Make it personal, or don't; dance party, toast a colleague, share a funny meme or picture. The possibilities are endless.

3 Tips For Getting The Most Out Of A Collaboration Tool

Try 'em all: Well, it may not be practical to try all of them out, I suggest looking into a few different ones to find the one that will best suit your needs. They each offer different features and are best used for different scenarios. Here is a list of a few that I've come across (in alphabetical order):

- Deskle
- Invision
- Miro
- Mural
- Stormboard
- Whimsical

Take time in advance to plan and prepare: Most of these tools have lots of functionality, templates and finnicky bits.

I find that my most productive sessions are the ones where I've taken time to think through the facilitation plan, organized the templates on my tool of choice, accommodated for different styles, different technology (desktop vs. mobile) and technology failures.

Consider how you will share the tool invite: Different tools have different subscription plans, and also different approaches to sharing or inviting additional participants. Take the time, in advance, to learn how your specific tool handles multiple participants.

Share video tutorials with your participants in advance: search on YouTube, the company website, or create your own.

Final Thoughts

I know it can be scary. I remember the first time I planned to use Mural for a workshop. I had used all of my political capital to convince a group of skeptics to trust me and forgo the traditional in-person workshop by using an approach that was not only new to them, but also entirely new to me. I was nervous and frankly, had a lot on the line. I didn't let that stop me. I took the time to get a 1:1 tutorial from a friend who knew the tools and technology well, and even invited her in to orient folks to the technology for the first time. I asked for grace and compassion. And, in the end, not only did we achieve our intended outcomes I was also able to convert a group of skeptics into remote collaboration advocates.

I urge you to leverage this opportunity. Embrace the fear and nerves. Be vulnerable and ask for patience. Be the champions within your teams and organizations for embracing remote collaboration. Think of this not as a stopgap, rather as a new way to engage and collaborate with people from near and far.

Go for it. I'm here for you!

About Janelle Mansfield

Janelle is an experienced executive and management consultant in the disciplines of customer experience, marketing, communications, change management and strategy. She is an early-adopter of technologies that foster better collaboration and engagement with customers, employees and stakeholders.

Her previous corporate and client-focused experience has elevated the business results and practices of leading companies in multiple industries, including IBM Canada, Canada Post, the University of Ottawa and Department of National Defense Canada. Janelle is known for her open and approachable leadership style, collaborative nature and strategic thinking.

While working with IBM Canada and their subsidiary ISM Canada, Janelle pioneered the use of Mural.co, a remote collaboration tool that replaces the need for in-person workshops. She has since gone on to deliver a dozen workshops and webinars on the topic of embracing remote collaboration tools for creating more immersive experiences.

Currently, Janelle lives her purpose and passion by helping leaders amplify their customer experiences for better business results through her consultancy, Amplified Customer Experience (*www.amplifiedcx.com*).

To find out how to best to leverage immersive and collaborative technologies in your organization, contact Janelle at *janelle@amplifiedcx.com.*

She also has video tutorials available on her YouTube channel:

http://www.youtube.com/c/AmplifiedCustomerExperience?sub_confirmation=1

Or, connect with her on *LinkedIn* (include the note: *Getting Immersive* in your connection request):

https://www.linkedin.com/in/janellemansfield/

How To *Flourish* Working From Home

Ian Hale

I think most of us want to be happy and yet experience ups and downs in life. I began my journey to understand what makes me happy, or unhappy, after a near fatal car accident.

In the early years of my life, though it seems chaotic to me now, I enjoyed a variety of jobs. Initially, I wanted to be a lawyer, instead I trained as a chef. At eighteen years old I was living and working in Amsterdam, then I returned to England and became a head chef of a hotel.

In a change of career, I sold advertising and developed sales training courses. I have started companies and had to close others. I have organised and run events for thousands of people in hundreds of locations. After my experience had been built, I ended up speaking at these events as a leadership consultant in culture and change.

To fulfil a desire to understand more about people and culture, I have travelled the world and visited over a hundred countries. I have coached some of the most successful leaders in the largest organisations across the globe and now find I am able to do that from the comfort of my home in the Devon countryside.

Into the bargain, I maintained a happy marriage to my wife

Ellie for 36 years, have two amazing sons and two wonderful grandchildren.

There have also been moments of deep depression and despair, caused by everything from my car accident and subsequent health issues to losing jobs and money worries. Not knowing what lay ahead in my future, I have even been unhappy enough to attempt to end my life.

With the benefit of hindsight, I now see that I was responsible for myself in all these situations. Though I didn't always realise it then, no event has been as bad as I thought it was at the time.

It's just that I didn't always see the opportunity nor have the resources to deal with it. This is what took me on this path to discover how to be happy.

When my grandchildren were born, I made a promise to them that I will do everything I can to create a world where communication between people is grounded in love and forgiveness with compassion at the core. Ever since, I have made it my purpose to help create and generate happiness, sense of fun and joy wherever I go.

The ancient Greek philosopher Aristotle described happiness as the central purpose to our lives. I love the fact that people like him had the time back then to think about happiness. I always thought they were busy fighting battles, building temples, worshipping gods, criticising leaders or surviving plagues. Maybe things haven't changed that much after all!

What Aristotle said was that we should focus on purpose, personal vitality, engaging in things which are meaningful, and spirituality. The neuroscientists of today agree that rather than focus on the end goal of happiness, 'spiritual mindfulness' may be found in Aristotle's steps to lead a happy and flourishing life.

Like a plastic bottle emptied of water we lose our strength if we don't keep filling ourselves up again. I am sharing the three practices that I have learned, and I hope will make the biggest difference to you when working on your own.

1. Breathe

Did you know that your body is designed to release toxins through the process of breathing?

If you're not breathing properly, you're unlikely to be eliminating toxins and your body system will be working harder to keep you well.

Do you remember the last time you were about to have an injection? You tense up your body, you hold your breath and wait for the prick of the needle. That feeling of anticipation, knowing pain is coming, prompts you to keep hold of that breath and if you are not careful you retain that awful feeling. As counterintuitive as it sounds, science suggests you breathe into the pain to help ease it. It's equally important to keep releasing any tension when working on your own.

Now, take a moment to feel your own breath. Don't force your breathing, instead take a deeper breath and then gently let that breath out. Keep on breathing. Were you aware of your breath before I said that? Most people are not. Notice what's happening. As your breath oxygenates your body and brain, any tensions or anxieties will begin to reduce.

Next, pay full attention to your breathing. Breathe slowly, deeply and purposefully five times. As you do, notice any places in your body that are feeling tight, then as you relax more, you might discover that this form of breathing brings clarity to certain things. Buddhists refer to this as a form of meditation allowing you to feel the sensations of the breath in and upon your body.

Maybe you didn't pick up this book to learn how to breathe, however when you're working alone or are isolated, tension can build up. In that isolation you can become constricted and that is when muscles in your body become tight, your breathing becomes shallow and you don't take in all the oxygen you need.

2. Be thankful.

Did you know that the part of the brain that worries is designed to help the body deal with difficult stuff and stress? Worry activates the brain's reward centre, strangely resulting in you feeling a little better. Both negative and positive emotions behave in a similar way, however it's the sustained worry, over time, that leaves us feeling uncomfortable and unhappy.

It may seem challenging in some situations you find yourself in, but something incredible happens in the brain when you are consciously and consistently thankful. All sorts of helpful chemicals kick in, similar to the medication prescribed by doctors for anti-depression.

Feeling gratitude lifts your mood and what's even more amazing, is if in the moment you're not feeling grateful, research shows that the very activity of searching for something to be grateful for activates the region of your brain that produces those helpful chemicals!

Having gratitude works positively on our brains, though few people consistently practice it. I write a daily morning and evening journal of what I am grateful for, what I appreciated about my day, or what I did well.

I recommend you simply do what I ask my clients to do when they arrive for a session:

"Ask yourself: what you are grateful for?"

3. Virtual Hugging

The biggest impact on our health is the quality of our relationships. My friend and colleague Berni always hugs me for nine seconds every time we meet. Whilst it may seem unnecessarily long, she tells me that science proves that when one fully surrenders to receive a hug, happy hormones including oxytocin, the love drug, are activated.

With colleagues like Berni I have always worked hard to maintain good relationships because the important people in our lives, be they spouses, partners, children, extended family, friends, work colleagues, clients or social communities, will all benefit and flourish the more we give to them.

Working from home can intensify the feeling of isolation so following this tried and tested method of virtual hugging will help you to recreate the benefits of physical hugging in all your interactions.

The most effective way to touch people emotionally is to acknowledge and appreciate them. You may feel embarrassed or uncomfortable when you are being acknowledged or when acknowledging someone else but trust me, afterwards you and your *buddy* will say it's a positive experience.

When you finish this chapter why not call or speak with someone. Tell them something heartfelt or appreciative. You don't need to give it any preamble. What could you acknowledge them for? Something they do well, something that you appreciate. Even a simple *thank you* to a client for doing business with you or to a colleague or co-worker for how responsive they are to your requests.

Don't leave it too late.

Two days before he passed, I told my father about something I was working on which was hugely important to me at the time. Given the circumstances, unsurprisingly, he didn't seem very responsive.

I said "Oh, of course, but I thought you'd be proud of me".

To which he replied, "But I've always been proud of you".

That was a shock to me because I didn't know that, and when I later told this to my mother she said, "Remember, Dad came from an environment where that level of expression was rarely displayed."

In that moment I truly understood how much he loved me and I'd waited over 30 years to hear it! It made me realise that I could spend the next 48 hours before his passing, telling him how much I loved and appreciated him!

Acknowledge those people now! Thank you, on behalf of my grandchildren's future.

About Ian Hale

Ian is a product of the stiff-upper-lip English middle-class system. This has given him a complex psychology which Ian has spent his life simplifying.

Ian shares his insights with everyone he interacts with, which can be challenging to those who are inexperienced at exposing their true self. This is especially true in the world of multinational corporates, where Ian has been engaged as a trusted coach and advisor to thousands of senior leaders. Ian has helped redefine their values and given them a purpose beyond bottom-line results. He challenges many, but Ian's charisma, humour and genuine care carry the participants over the hurdles.

Ian lives and breathes an infectious spirit of excitement, energy, and enthusiasm. He has been told he has an uncanny ability to brighten people's day, and loves hearing from others to do just that.

Website: https://elantlc.co.uk

Email: mail@elantlc.co.uk

LinkedIn: https://www.linkedin.com/in/ian-hale-elantlc/

How To Overcome The Various Challenges Of Working From Home

Michelle D Harris

Many people around the world are working remotely for the first time at the moment as a way to combat the coronavirus outbreak. This brings its own set of challenges and struggles for business and home workers but there are also many benefits. The benefits are...

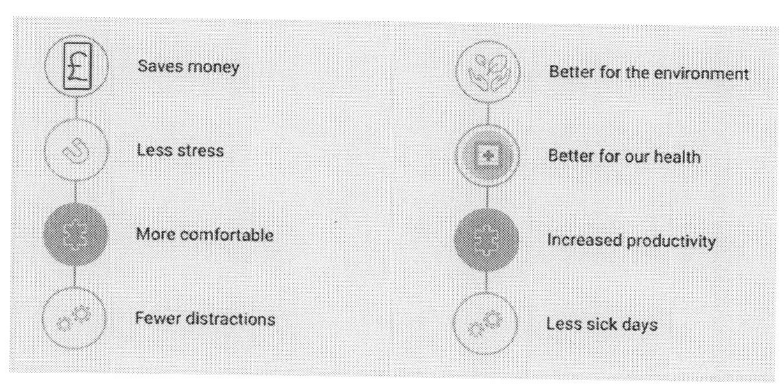

In the old days we used to call working from home telecommuting and it wasn't very common at all, now it seems to be called remote working – which for me conjurors up people working on beaches and VW vans on the road. However it seems to just mean, working away from the office.

remote working

noun [U]

UK US https://dictionary.cambridge.org/

HR, WORKPLACE

a situation in which an employee works mainly from home and communicates with the company by email and telephone:

As I said to tackle this Pandemic right now some people are being told to work from home if they can and the point is many people are finding themselves in a situation that they were not expecting and that they had not prepared for.

Just not being prepared can cause many more challenges that it would do normally. There is plenty of advice out there about working from home, but I've already found that during lockdown brings a completely new set of challenges

Be Flexible

It's most important that everyone is flexible and understanding with the changes, which not only working from home brings but working from home during a lockdown and that includes other members of the family, teams and leaders.

It's not a one size fits all situation when it comes to working from home. There are many different factors to take into consideration. You can follow a few set guidelines which really can help but it is important to remember to be calm, breathe and above all be flexible. Your day may not always go to plan and that is okay.

Over the last 30 years I have spent 17 of them working from home. Each decade has brought different challenges to me, and the last few weeks even more of them, so I'm keen to share my experiences with others who might find it difficult to work from home.

Challenges can be:

- Children at home
- Partners at home
- Other adults at home
- Feeling a lack of community
- Loss of productivity
- Guilty feelings that you aren't getting enough done
- Worried that you are getting enough done but you have to do more because no one knows
- Loneliness
- Claustrophobia
- Depression
- Weight gain
- Keeping healthy
- Eating the right foods

One of the most important things is our mental health; structure and routine can go a long way to help us with that and my guidelines will help with this.

Health of course is another very important factor which is sometimes over looked. You will be surprised how much exercise you get actually travelling to and from work and walking around the office, which you won't get anymore.

Not Home Alone

Often people find that they are lonely when they are working from home, but during this time of the Corona virus lockdown many are finding that there are too many people at home.

Other adults at home might also need to be remote working, while others might not be working.

Having people at home in your house is a challenge, I am coming from a place of experience here, I've always had my place to myself all day, so I'm having to create a different schedule and set of systems that I have managed for 10 years.

Schedules

Schedules are needed but we must adapt to our situation to suit.

Most importantly best thing to do is not to panic! Don't try to do it all at once, we will fit it in, everyone will relax into it.

Remember not everyone finds it easy to work from home and not everyone wants to work from home and some won't ever get used to it. We are all different, and that's okay.

However I do feel that if you can follow these rules or guidelines in a way that suits you, it will provide you with a good foundation.

Loneliness

If you are used to working in an office with a big team, suddenly finding yourself working from home on your own might seem a bit daunting, lonely and even isolating.

I am only of the lucky ones who do not get lonely – I embrace my social self but there are many small business owners or remote workers that do suffer with loneliness.

I've always been a big networker so I have lots of people to chat to online if I need to, and I feel this is why I've have not suffered.

So, find a place online to call home you can go for a chat now and then, especially if you don't have a team to work with. If you are looking for just that place, please do contact me, as I have some spaces in my networking groups. Some members are other authors in this book. No one needs to be alone!

To stay in touch is even easier now than when I started working from home, it sometimes feels that technology has advanced in such a way to push us into remote working.

Working from home also saves time, we get extra time that we lost travelling into work and for some people that could be 2/3 hours per day! So think of that extra time you can have with family or spending time on your hobbies.

So back to the tips, these work for me, so you might find some of them useful especially when just starting out.

Top Tips For Remote Working

Set Work Hours

Have set work hours, its best for your sanity. Depending on what your boss/client wants, you don't really need to work 9-5 if those were your office hours. If you are able to be flexible then do – work it around others, work in the quiet times or your most productive or creative times.

Whatever schedule you do choose I think it's important to stick to those times, so your colleges clients or family know that you are at work. Don't be surprised if people start asking you to do household errands when you want to work if not.

Personal Jobs / Housework

Don't be tempted to think you can put the washing on or do the washing up at any time. You'll be surprised how much this personal time takes up work time, and they need to be separate. You can use your lunch break for that; make sure you *do* have a lunch hour (even 30mins) to have a break, maybe a walk, and some healthy food too.

Time Management Is Very Important

There are a few tactics you can put in to place to help with time management. There are some things you need to avoid and some that you will need to learn to manage or focus on.

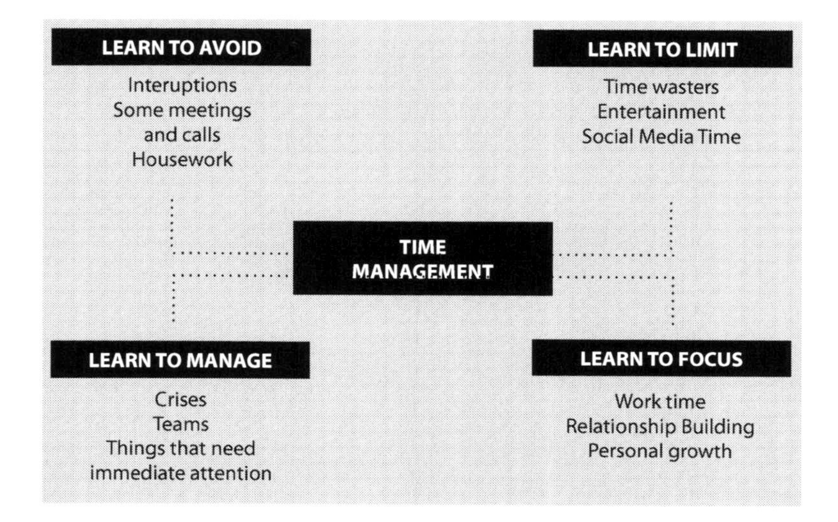

Stick To A Morning Routine

In the morning, get up, shower, get dressed and even put makeup on (if you wear it) like you would normally for going to work, that way you are always ready for the impromptu Zoom meeting or Google hangout with the boss and you FEEL ready for work, your brain likes to know you are ready to work also.

Make use of apps tools available to help to manage time and get things done.

Technology now, has grown for us to choose whenever app or platform we want, many of them are free too.

- Use a planner or calendar to write down deadlines or to block out time for meetings
- Have a to-do list – there's an app for that – Todoist

- Keep a track of ongoing work, for just your or your team with Trello or maybe Slack
- Track your time with Toggl
- Keep in touch with colleagues and share work using Slack or Discord.

To name just a few, have a Google and see what tools are available for what you are trying to achieve

Remote Working Guidelines

Create A Permanent Workspace

Have an area that you can call your office. This way other people in the house know that when you are at your desk you are at work and not to be disturbed. It helps you also you know that when you leave that area, you are not at work and can rest. This could be a spare room or just the corner of a room somewhere but not the bedroom, you will feel like you are always at work.

Relying on working at the kitchen table, or on the sofa, isn't really a great idea, there can be distractions. If you have to just for a few weeks, you can be flexible but you will need to also have a great time table. As not having an office set up doesn't provide you with a line between work and home life, and your brain won't know it's time to work. If you can get a desk and find a corner of a room to put it or if you are lucky enough to have a spare room you can call your office.

Calendar planning

Of course time management is pretty important, and you will find it easier with these two strategies Calendar planning and time blocking.

This doesn't need to be limited to work – you can put everything on it, so you know exactly how much time you have in during the day.

If you are working with a team, or have many clients - then calendar planning is god save. It can let everyone know when you are available, like I said being available for that short notice meeting. Communicating with colleagues is a must, but they must also know when you are working and when you are not. You don't want to get into being available 24/7 that's not good for anyone's mental health.

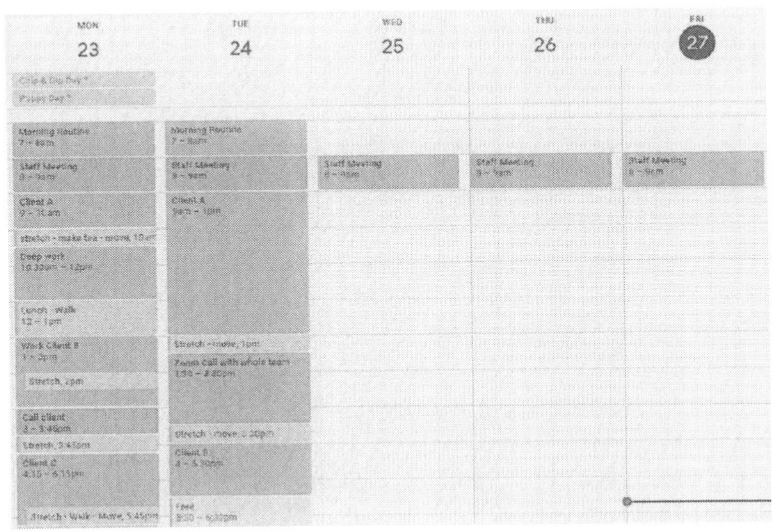

Blocking Time

Blocking time in advance shows others when people can get hold of you or when you are at your desk working.

Print it out and put it above your desk for family to read or put it in the Slack group that your business is using to keep connected.

It's even helpful if you work alone and you want to make sure you keep your time for what it should be for when people say, Let's jump on a call, you can see at a glance how your day/week looks.

Messenger Apps For Realtime Messaging

I feel that Slack.com or the WhatsApp applications are essential for keeping in touch when working from home.

Having an instant message system that is always on, on a status update that says *I'm available now* is a good idea if people need to get hold of you quickly – and you don't want to keep getting stuck on the phone. Instant messages are much quicker and simpler to deal with.

That way people know they can contact you to get an immediate response like in the office. For instant messages, you could use Skype, WhatsApp, Discord, Slack app/platforms like are perfect for that reason. You can turn on notifications @ messages to your name so you can respond right away. This way your team, boss or client can know what you are doing and that they can get hold of you at short notice.

What Might This Mean For The Future

Amazon, Google, and Apple have measures in place to allow remote working for their staff during this Pandemic and many businesses are also changing to have their events and conferences virtually. If this businesses find that this all went well for them, we might not only save lives but this may change the way work for ever.

I really do hope these tips helped you, I am usually always on Twitter if you want to connect with me for more tips please do @michelledh

About Michelle D Harris

Michelle D Harris is a Social Media Manager, Community Manager, Virtual Engagement Specialist and Content Creator, with experience that includes 30 years' working in digital technology, marketing and building communities online.

She loves to work with people who are trying to make a difference in the world or to people lives, start-ups women leaders, life coaches, and entrepreneurs.

Her passion is to help people to achieve their goals by increasing brand awareness, creating engagement , increasing following, building communities and essentially bringing in more business

https://www.linkedin.com/in/michelleharrissocial

https://twitter.com/michelledh

https://www.instagram.com/michelledh/

https://www.michelleharris.social/

Working in Barbara

James Barrington-Brown

Ok, what does the title conjure up in your mind? Many different things I'm sure, but Barbara is actually the name of my motorhome - well that's what I call her anyhow, the manufacturers named her Swift Lifestyle 696 - which just isn't that catchy. I'm currently on Barbara version three.

Now, for clarity and to paint the right picture, a motorhome isn't a mobile home, which paradoxically, is normally static with plant pots by the door, a tiny plastic picket fence around it, often gnomes are present in great numbers, well why wouldn't you! A motorhome has an engine, wheels and is actually well, *mobile*.

I have owned motorhomes for just over 16 years, and enjoyed working from them immensely. Depending on the type of work you are trying to do, you can relocate somewhere appropriate, like the countryside for peace and quiet. Or if you need to meet someone, take your office with you. After all, you have everything you need, water, fridge, hob, kettle, loo etc. and oh yeah, it's a bit different and it's fun. Work should be fun. No, let's rewind that, there shouldn't be *work* at all. Get your life right, and the word *work* can be removed from your vocabulary, it's just a structured part of a life you enjoy.

But yes, agreed, we have to call it work, as that is the norm, but it can and should be enjoyable, if it isn't then you need to change things.

Using a motorhome as a study really does bring reality to the words remote working. Allowing you to be as remote as you like, depending on your communication and data requirements being available, of course.

Most of us have experienced great ideas whilst we are on holiday with fresh air, sunshine, calmness, nature. All of which contribute to our minds relaxing and seeing bigger pictures. Well jumping in Barbara, is like being on holiday every day.

Yes, I confess. I have a nice house, with a study, and I also have an office. However, my first choice is Barbara every time. Even now, I'm writing this piece whilst sitting in Barbara with the glorious March sunlight streaming in. I glance up now and again to enjoy the vista of flowers and watching the busy spring wildlife do its thing.

It is easy to forget that humans need to be connected to the planet to help maintain mental health. Which is why being able to look out the many windows and skylights certainly makes that connection with nature easy. Along with the ability to change that scenery. Fancy the beach? Rolling hills? You got it. As simple as just turning the key, and away you go.

Anyway, that's enough about motorhomes. Wherever your particular selected workspace is, you need certain elements to keep sane and healthy, natural daylight, a view outside, good communication tools along with connectivity, some peace, a comfortable chair being some of the key ones.

Most of us work best when we have defined the times for doing tasks. Without timetables or deadlines, things just seem to slip by, sometimes for weeks on end. Having a timetable has the added benefit of giving us a boost when we can tick that item off. Another success hurrah! It's important to achieve not fail. This can be achieved by developing a timetable that works for you. When to look at the news, IM notifications, posts, emails and this list goes on. There have been days where I've randomly looked at a lot of things in succession, but have got to the end of the day feeling disappointed due to the lack of achievement. Missing the day's intentions.

Everyone is different. For me, I like to get ready for work, showered, dressed in whatever feels comfortable and appropriate for the day ahead. Follow this up with breakfast. Only then does my working day start. If I'm going to be precise, my tasks start at this point. I would have already looked at instant messages, emails, tweets etc.

Having a TV in a room where you are working isn't a good idea. The temptation to switch it on and *just* catch the news can be overwhelming. TVs, are not your friend. They are time stealers. These days there's little excuse to want to watch something live. Most of us have catch-up TV, available on a variety of channels. Why not watch it in the evening, whilst being content with your day's achievements.

Availability - how should this be handled. Do let family, friends and colleagues know when you are available to talk. For instance, with your family it could be that your door is open when you are available as this is a visual way of communication. With friends, colleagues and clients it could be you have *do not disturb* set on your instant messaging. Reducing the amount of notifications, especially sounds, can have a huge benefit. This form of contact can be instantly distracting. If you're brave enough, log out of unnecessary apps and sites. This system can be adopted, and you do need to let people know the rules. When it's ok to contact you is vital. Otherwise you will get disturbed regardless of your do not disturb settings. Put the boundaries in place and politely remind them of the rules when suitable opportunities arise.

Tasks - Google Tasks alongside Google Calendar help guide me through the day. I find I do need a guide. At the end of each day, I can then check through the tasks, moving any uncompleted ones to the following day. This is followed up by always putting a time on each one, even if it's for a future date. Timed prompts are useful as they spread themselves over the day in Google Calendar, as opposed to having a bunch listed out of sight under a *more* link. If the tasks are building up on any given day, I then see and know I either have to get through tasks quicker or I have to reset my thinking. As somewhere there's a mismatch between what I believe my abilities are and my real capabilities. More often than not, they don't quite match up to how good I think I am. There are always uncompleted tasks. How could that possibly be?

Optimism - yes must be that. Tasks can also be used to allow for having a break. Get in, that's a double win. Reminded to have a break and you get to tick it off as complete once the break is over.

So as mentioned above, I find trying to put too many tasks into a day can lead to a feeling of being overwhelmed, but that's daft as I'm the one who put them in, so be realistic as to how many tasks you can complete in a day.

Completing a task and putting a tick beside it is satisfying. In contrast, seeing the daily list slowly expand isn't satisfying at all. Quite frankly, it's demoralising.

So be realistic as to what you can achieve, as you can always select a future task and do it today. Ticking items off is pleasing. It might only produce a few endorphins, but it has a positive effect on your brain. Certainly, much better than not succeeding. Don't set yourself up to fail, success gives you momentum, which creates more success. Like the saying goes, if you want something done, give it to a busy person, they are flying for a reason.

Video calls and conferences - Zoom is currently flavour of the month. As a conference call admin, it's always a good idea to email and/or text a reminder of the details 30 minutes, to an hour, before the meeting is due to take place. It really is amazing how many people forget. Have all the details in front of you and ideally you would have already created the conference group contacts in your phone and on email, making it easy to send out messages quickly. Having a back-up option is vital, like an old-school phone-based system, as these are far more reliable and tend to just work. By having an email ready to go with the alternative system connection details means you can quickly switch systems if the need arises. Sharing the meeting details, which includes your house style can be particularly helpful, especially if there's a number of people joining the call. A typical house style might be for everyone to be on mute, with the admin controlling proceedings asking specific people to talk, whilst participants ask the admin via chat or by holding a hand up if they want to speak. The chat feature in most video conferencing software is useful for messaging an individual, or the whole group, without interrupting the person talking. There's nothing worse than everyone trying to talk over the top of one another. Worse still, only the more forceful people on the call dominating the proceedings. Who hasn't been on one of those types of calls? Sometimes the quiet person has the most important things to say, and it's via the admin who controls things properly that the quiet person gets their turn to speak.

Having a work/life balance is much talked about. So being able to choose your place to operate is better for having a balanced life. Remember, we removed the concept of *work* earlier.

Not everyone wants a motorhome as an office. But don't you now want to hire one and give it a go? Try it. You'll love it. What would you call yours?

About James Barrington-Brown

James is an experienced businessman who has been founding and building companies for 37 years, of which the last 22 years being in the tech sector. He has gained in-depth knowledge from running many businesses.

James has successfully sold several of his enterprises. James has been interviewed live on the BBC as a technology thought leader and had his products promoted by Martin Lewis, the consumer champion which assisted in over 2.5m of his smartphone apps being downloaded. James was also early in the crypto currency space, mining Bitcoin and Litecoin since 2013.

His main business currently is Barritel, a telecommunications provider.

Website - www.barritel.com

LinkedIn - inkedin.com/in/james-barrington-brown-1882481a/

Twitter - @JamesBB123

Working Alone – Together

Susan Popoola

If you've suddenly found yourself suddenly compelled to work from home as a result of a crisis such as the corona virus pandemic, it's possible that it's come as a shock to your system, leaving you trying to work out what this means in practical terms. Beyond the distractions of what's going on in the wider environment, how do you make this work so that you are able to both continue to generate an income and derive the satisfaction from doing so through those things that normally motivate you to get up each day to go out and work?

The first thing to say is you are not alone. You are one of the many millions that will have suddenly found yourself in this position; joining millions of other professionals that already work successfully from home, inclusive of people that have gone on to develop some of the most successful businesses in the world.

I recognise that starting to work from home at this time is a bit different from the norm as you may have had little time to plan. None the less, whether you work independently or as part of a wider organisation, I believe people will understand if it takes a little bit of time for you to get things up and running smoothly.

I would suggest that once you've taken the time to breathe, sit down to review your commitments – are they still deliverable; do you have to change the format and can originally timeframes be met? Then communicate, communicate, communicate – from my experience, communication is more important than ever so make sure you also have some basic equipment – such as a laptop and a webcam with access to a video app such as Zoom.

Key then is what you're going to do going forward and how you are going to do it whether working as part of an organisation or working independently. If you are part of a larger organisation, my hope is that you will be involved in discussions about the business – what is delivered (and how deliverables may change); how things now need to be delivered at least for an interim period and how this impacts people's roles and responsibilities. Indeed you may be leading on or need to initiate such conversations.

If you are an independent like me, then it's something you may need to do independently, at least in the first instance.

I've worked as an independent for well over 20 years working as a Talent and Organisation Development Strategist, working with a variety of organisations large and small. I also run projects supporting young people and I've written a few books. This means that although I've historically gone out to deliver on projects and to attend meetings; my home has been my office base. Even though I work independently, I've never felt alone as I have a very good network inclusive of associates, advisers, past colleagues, clients and friends. A good network to me, is one of the most fundamental elements of successfully working from home without feeling lonely or alone.

Work for me as with most people, is a fundamental part of my live. In most cases, not only does it provide us with income it fulfils broader purposes in our lives which will vary from one person to another: providing a sense of fulfilment or achievement; status; the ability to contribute to something and perhaps make a difference; the opportunity to use our skillsets; to innovative or create or what have you. I believe that working from home should not change this even if products/services or the delivery methods need to be adapted.

As a result of the pandemic, I've taken the opportunity to review the work that I do and how I deliver it. As in other times when I'm making changes to what I'm doing, I've had conversations with a few different people to help my thinking and understand the landscape; I've put some thoughts together on what needs to changed and have discussed my plans with a few key people to ensure my plans are practical. I've then gone out to test the market, constantly keeping what I do under review.

If you're working from home you want to be just as productive and profitable as you would be the case if you were working in an office – if not more so. You also want it to be a pleasant or even fun experience. With the clarity around what you do and how you deliver, your working environment and protocols then become key, taking account of your values, the culture you want to adopt; legislation, the environment and security issues.

We are all different, so I'd say the one crucial rule is that our setup works for us; the people we work with and deliver to, as also the people that we may live with. There are those that are concerned about working from home because they believe it must be lonely or comes with too many distractions. It doesn't have to be lonely; it depends on the nature of your work (as some work is naturally more interactive than others); how you structure your day and your interactions.

Personality types also play apart; by nature an introvert may be happy beavering away in a corner, but may procrastinate over getting on the phone to communicate. On the other hand, an introvert may want to spend all his or her time communicating and be resistant to doing other things.

It's therefore useful get to know yourself better and understand what your naturally drawn to. One good way to do this will be to take a psychometric test which will tell you not only more about yourself and how you're naturally inclined to interact, but will also enable you to better understand how to interact with others with different personality types from yours. There are quite a number of available profiling tools, the main one that I use when working with both adults and young people that I'm working with is Clarity4D.

Establish a structure for your day which takes account of both you as an individual and the people living with you/that you have responsibilities for. Sometimes client delivery determines the structure of my day, otherwise I typically start my work day with a morning walk to get myself in a positive mind frame and signal to my brain that I'm going into work mode; to make the switch some people put on "work" clothes. I spend the morning writing, developing materials and doing other types of desk-top work. I try to discipline myself not to review social media until lunch time as it can be quite consuming and distracting. Post lunch I tend to focus on my interactions with the rest of the world. In the evening I may switch on the television almost as an indicator that the official work day is over. Others may change clothes or move from their dedicated workspace to a different part of the house. On occasion, I might go out and socially – during a lockdown, there's always the option of doing so online with the various technologies available.

I typically end the day reflecting on the day, highlighting even the smallest of achievements; setting out my objectives for the next day and perhaps doing a bit of reading to clear my head for the next day. Objectives and achievements are important to me as I focus on outputs rather than hours worked. This does mean that I have had to learn to be realistic about my expectations for myself. I believe there's a greater satisfaction in being able to say what I achieved in a day then how many hours I work.

I also recommend to employers that they focus on employee outcomes rather than hours. This is especially important for professionals working from home whereby some professionals are combining work with caring responsibilities – some activities which may need to take place during the working day. Key then for individuals with caring responsibilities or just living with others is to establish an agreed routine with clear boundaries agreed with those you live with and those you work with as appropriate.

Once more I will mention the importance of communication – both one to one and team communications within an organisation and communications with key advisors and associates for the independent. There are so many tools available from the good old fashion phone, WhatsApp, Microsoft Team and Zoom. There's really no excuse not to communicate, but key is to find the most appropriate methods of communications for you and the people to interact with; ensure not to overload people with communications; and manage expectations in terms of responses.

Above all else enjoy working from home, it might take some getting used to, but it can be very fulfilling – enabling your to be more productive with an additional flexibility and time to do other things you enjoy. Remember working from home, you may be alone, but if you communicate you will be alone together.

#Selah

About Susan Popoola

Susan is an award winning consultant specialising in Talent Management, Inclusion and Engagement; a Community Activist with a deep-rooted belief in human value; a published author of books exploring the world in which we live in; and a Public Speaker.

She runs Mosaic Fusions which takes Human Value Optimisation Approach to working with organisations to develop highly productive and fulfilling workplaces that reflect the rich diversity of the society that we live in.

She also runs Mosaic Wise works to engage teenagers and young adults in education, the workplace and wider society through a series of activities and programmes inclusive of talks, workshops, roundtables, profiling and development tools; and one to one coaching and mentoring support.

www.MosaicWorld.live

LinkedIn: linkedin.com/in/SusanPopoola

Twitter: SusanPopoola

Instagram: SusanPopoola

Punch Above Your Weight From Home

Bob Hayward

One cold Tuesday, the 5th February 1991, my last proper job went pop. While my company could have survived that recession our holding company could not. Having lost £100 million on a property development project the Banks closed the holding company and all seven subsidiaries. Then began my love affair with working from home. Ah, no. I did stupidly, accept one last job as Sales Director for another firm. It only lasted a few weeks because I fired the owner's son for being a very naughty chap at work and then was promptly fired myself by the owner, his Mum, for not following procedure...

Then began my love affair with remote working.

Home, at that time, was a five-bedroom house in Swindon. My first home office was a desk, a wooden chair, a phone and a filing cabinet in the utility room. A huge personal computer filled the desk and the printer sat on top of a four-drawer filing cabinet.

I was in my element, starring at a blank wall, surrounded by two cats, four children, aged four to eleven, and a wife who was wondering when a real job would come along and save her, and me, from this weird situation.

Now in March 2020, I look back over 29 years of working from home, successfully, from where I've worked all over the UK,

Europe and as far East as Sri Lanka for great organisations big and small.

Working from home does not mean your business has to be small, or one without significant impact. If you approach running a business remotely with the right mindset, network, knowledge and tools you can punch above your weight and often beat bigger competitors to large and profitable work.

How do you punch above your weight?

Set Up A Registered Company With A Business Address And Answerphone Service

Why? Because those making the buying decisions for larger or longer pieces of work want a sense of security. They do not want risk getting a bill from the Government for paying a person as self-employed when they should have treated them as an employee. Those in procurement want to buy from a legal and credible entity, as well as a talented person. In many industries sub-contractors and the self-employed are still perceived differently from an officially registered company.

You might wish to argue against that perception, but I'd advise you to save your breath. If you want to win more profitable work, which longer and larger projects often are, set up as a Registered Company. Set up a real virtual business address, not a PO Box. This inexpensive service means your website and business card can look the part. Find a telephone answering service. My business phone number has been answered by a professional team of receptionists for years. They quickly learned to represent my brand, knew the type of calls to reject or accept and got to know my clients. None of my clients have ever questioned who answers the phone.

From the very beginning my company looked and felt like a proper business, a credible entity, not just a talented one-man band. This helped open doors at companies big and small and helps close sales repeatedly.

Separate The Oil From The Water

If you work remotely you must figure out where to work.

Are you going to set up in a spare room? The kitchen? The bedroom? The living room?

Suddenly that space, the lighting, the heating, the noise, who else uses that space and when comes into play. In an office environment everyone is using the same space for the same purpose. Move the office into the kitchen and now there are two completely different uses for that room. Oil and water rarely mix so think carefully about where to set up your office. Create boundaries between work life and personal life; find ways to use the office space for just work. Ways to cover up the papers when work time is over, or ways you can quickly and easily shut it all away.

With four children, two cats, and a house-proud wife taking over part of the lounge or dining room for part of the day was never going to work. I needed peace and quiet to work and I did not want to be forced to move things because someone else wanted that room.

At times my office has been in a utility room with the washing machine, a converted spare bedroom, and a converted attic. Even in 1991, with a computer, a phone and a filing cabinet I could run the business. I didn't need anything more. My office was organised by frequency of use. If I used an item all the time, I kept it on or in my desk, items used less frequently were in the filing cabinet and things I rarely needed were in the garage. These days, all I need is a laptop, my mobile phone and Wi-Fi because my filing is all in the cloud. So, while I still have a home office, with a two-drawer filing cabinet and a printer, I also have an office in my gym, any coffee shop with Wi-Fi, any hotel, airport or train.

Boundaries are also about time. Learn to switch work, the mobile and the laptop off. Learn to switch on time with the loves of your life.

My daily routine has always been an important part of my boundaries. Six hours sleep. Up at 5am, read, pray, work out, shower, breakfast, plan and work. Yes, get shaved, showered and dressed for business. I always feel more motivated when I dress for work. I also learned to create ideal templates a long time ago listening to Charles Hobbs the time management predecessor to Stephen Covey. An ideal day, an ideal week and an ideal month. A perfect office-based Monday, Tuesday working with clients, the perfect office-based Wednesday, Thursday working with clients. Friday a perfect day out with the love of my life while our four cherubs were at school. Saturday a great day out with the cherubs and Sunday a great day at Church and with friends for meals. I learned that lesson the hard way, as a workaholic who came back one week early from the two-week family holiday because the business needed me. The same business the Banks closed six months later in February 1991.

If It Is Below Your Hourly Rate Pay Someone Else To Do It

We either live in the flame of our candle, or in the wax. If you do tasks in your flame, you are using your talents, your best skills and qualities, you are alive, you give energy and you receive energy. When you do tasks in your wax you beat yourself up. You might be OK at the task, but you feel drained and demotivated by the thought of it.

In my first year of running my business from home there was a harsh recession on. I did not generate a huge turnover so I could not take much cash out of the business. The cash was not there. I did everything. I made my own appointments, I was the salesperson, delivered the work, raised the invoice, chased for payment, did the accounts and quarterly tax return.

Even then I could earn £250 to £650 per day. It took me a year to realise that doing the accounts was stopping me generating sales and that a bookkeeper could do them much faster and more accurately in a third of the time and at a fraction of the cost. Now I avoid tasks below my client day-rate.

Can you outsource tasks to someone, who will do a better job, faster and at a lower cost? Yes. Then delegate those tasks with some goals, key measures or a service standard and go do something more useful, enjoyable and profitable.

Your Knowledge And Your Network Are Your Wealth

Your knowledge and your network are your true wealth provided you develop them, nurture and leverage them. Working remotely through multiple recessions taught me the importance of networking. I learned most about networking from three people, Thomas and Penny Power who created Ecademy, the original LinkedIn, and Roger Hamilton of Wealth Dynamics. My network, in good times and bad has been my second-best new business channel, only topped by repeat business. Plus, all my sub-contractors, associates and suppliers have come from networking.

A BMW project had 32 associates in the delivery team, all from that network. The key is to give value and time to those in your network, to build trust and to learn the strengths of as many people as you can. Collecting business cards or adding people to your LinkedIn profile is not networking. If you don't know, like and trust someone they are unlikely to have the same feelings about you and they are not going to share the contents of their wallet with you. Their wealth, or wallet, is their network and knowledge.

Your knowledge is a vital part of your wealth, it is part of your uncommon advantage over your competition, as important as growing the size and developing the trust across your network.

What I get paid for now I could not have done back in 1991. Back then I subscribed to a monthly Nightingale Conant audio series. While I didn't have time to read books, it was easy to listen to seminars when driving or travelling. Whether car, train or plane those vehicles have been my university. Now Audible is my go-to source of learning. At least one book per month. There are few top-quality books on leadership, selling skills or business development theories that I've not read. It is rare anyone can mention a business theory or model that I do not know. Usually it is me suggesting new high-quality ideas and models to others.

While I am a remote worker, I am not remote from the wisdom and friendship of other talented people. To leverage both you must engage whole heartedly with people. Offer to help them, to give of your time, knowledge and network, ask for help, ask for opinions, ask for referrals and mot importantly to ask for a coffee. Habitually meet up with one person over coffee each day that you are not with a client. That way you can meet two to three people each week, some for the first time, some repeats, some associates, some prospects, some clients, some suppliers and yes some just friends. Do remember you have friends. The intentions with all such meetings are to build trust, learn about them and offer to help – free. Never to sell. While counterintuitive I have found that the more I give out the more that comes back and generally via a roundabout route.

So, there are my four top tips to building a profitable business as a remote worker.

- Set up as a registered business, with a real business address and a telephone answering service
- Set up boundaries, physically and with your schedule. Keep work separate from the other important parts of your home and life
- Outsource tasks that can be done at a higher quality, more quickly and a lower cost than by you

- Do something to develop and leverage your network and knowledge consistently. Learn every day. Build trust and understanding with two or three people each week

About Bob Hayward

Bob Hayward, a Christian, a father to four, grandad to five (so far) and a Spurs fan; if you can cope with those facts then you will get on well with him.

He is a catalyst for change to those who want a business breakthrough, a best-selling author and popular international speaker. Having started seven successful businesses, of which he still runs two, he now loves using his experience and the skills developed along the way to make growth happen for others - sometimes as a Non-Executive Director, or a Growth Consultant or as a Senior Executive Coach.

He has designed and delivered numerous mission-critical internal communication initiatives, employee engagement projects and skill development programmes for companies like Vodafone, BMW, and Skype. Feedback on his work is high in both levels of delegate satisfaction and of tangible business improvements.

Contact him at

https://www.linkedin.com/in/bobhayward/

Read more from Bob at

https://www.bemoreeffective.com/blog/

How To Be Productive When Working From Home - A Young Professional's Perspective

Safa Arif, Financial Services Professional

Having recently graduated from University, I envisioned my first *real job* as a young professional to be in a bustling office. This expectation was based on what we are shown on TV; people in suits rushing around, on important phone calls, trying to get deals done. The reality is that the modern age requires us to be able to work from home as employers and entrepreneurs need flexible working methods. As someone who has just left the higher education system, this has been a tough adjustment. Being in control of your time and managing your workload without colleagues or seniors supporting you can be a challenge.

There is sometimes a negative stigma attached to those that work from home as some believe they are less productive than those who work from an office. However, this is not true. Working from home requires a different level of dedication and motivation. I have realised that the biggest issue many of us face when working from home is that we can become our own worst enemy by limiting our productivity levels.

Having spent the last year trying different approaches, I now feel I have a way that works for me and my employer. In this chapter, I will share the methods I use to get the most out of my workday no matter the location. These methods give me a structure to my day and have delivered positive results for me and I hope they will help you achieve the same.

1. What is your Routine?

The foundation of working from home starts with your routine. Many people take each day as it comes, deciding how to approach the day as and when issues occur and fitting them in when they have a free minute. This is a highly ineffective way of working as without setting yourself objectives (or a simple to-do list), how can you measure whether your day has been successful or not?

Start by planning your week on a high-level basis. Before the week begins, I write a to-do-list and prioritise the items I need to work on based on what I have learnt from Stephen Covey's *Urgent and Important Matrix*. This will help you to plan your week by understanding those tasks that require your immediate attention and the tasks that can be pushed back. This will free up time to tackle any distractions that arise. To increase my productivity, I revisit the list at the end of each workday to see how I can plan for the following and decide which items I am going to attack.

Safa's Tasklist : Week Ending 6th March 2020	**Urgent** (Time sensitive)	**Not Urgent**
Important (Commercially sensitive)	• Complete customer complaints review • Prepare Project Alpha reporting deck	• Arrange session to brainstorm ideas for shorter approvals of B-19 forms • Book in review calls with regional brokers to analyse their numbers from last month
Non-Important	• Feedback on James proposal for new business opportunities • Do plan for next week • Work on my Personal Development Plan	• Complete my expenses • Complete weekly reading for Chartered Institute of Banking

Pretend you are going to the office. Make sure you wake up on time, have your breakfast or exercise, even change into work clothes before you get to your desk. People often think working from home allows them to have a relaxed approach to working practises however this is the wrong mindset to have. You are setting the tone to be at a disadvantage to someone who would be going into the office so make sure you start work on time.

2. Fail To Plan, Plan To Fail

Commit to doing more than maybe achievable. Working from home can be demotivating as you can be left to your own devices as no-one is watching you. When you have a to-do-list of five items, you may only achieve three as you will allow distractions to come in the way. But if you set targets to stretch yourself of ten items, you may actually complete the five you initially set out to do. This is how I have gradually improved my productivity levels by challenging myself past my own psychological boundaries.

Complete household tasks beforehand. You would not make your lunch from scratch in the office or do your laundry so why are you letting these tasks interrupt your home office workday? Do these things before you get into your *working time*. Separating your personal and professional life is important as otherwise you never really get either done to a satisfactory level.

Communicate expectations with your household. People can become the biggest distraction when working from home. The people you live with would not regularly call you during office hours to chat or ask you to run their errands, so do not allow them to do so during your home office hours. Make sure there is no opportunity for them to distract you during meetings and disrupt your concentration.

3. The Modern-Day Distractions

Put your personal device away. As Millennials, it has become normal for us to scroll down four Social Media timelines or binge-watch the latest crime documentary on Netflix and lose two hours of the day. I used to find myself getting drawn to my phone to check a message or read a tweet. When I am in the office, I would never do this, due to social judgement, so when I work from home, I put away my personal devices to avoid temptation.

Restrict yourself during working hours. You can use your phone's applications to help you here. I use Screen Time to measure and tell me how much time I have used on each app - it can be scary when you see the reality. Whilst mobile devices are important to a modern-day professional, some of the apps on your device are reducing your productivity.

Build breaks into your day. Just like you would go for a break in the office, during the day plan for coffee and lunch breaks to allow yourself to do other things like maybe catch a show or go onto your social media.

4. Understand Your Personal Well Being

Work when you are most productive. This is one of the big advantages of being able to work from home. People are different, some are early risers, whilst some work better later in the day. Working from home allows you to be more flexible in how you do your work. I know some colleagues who love taking their kids to school in the morning and then they get down to work. They say it gives them peace of mind and makes them more focussed when they are allowed this flexibility.

Take breaks away from the workspace. Outside! It can become very easy to spend your whole day at your desk and let work consume you. Whether it is for a run, to walk the dog or grabbing some lunch, fresh air helps to reset your mind for the rest of the day.

Focus on your Social Interaction. When I am working from home, I can sometimes go without speaking to anyone for the whole day and this can become socially isolating. To avoid this, schedule calls with colleagues throughout the day to discuss your daily agenda or brainstorm ideas that will help you get a different perspective.

5. Finishing On A High

Set a finish time and try to stick to it. When you are in the office, people can be waiting for 5 pm so they can get out of the door, but when working from home these boundaries can become blurred and affect our work-life balance. Aiming to log off at a certain time not only gives me personal time but also ensures work is completed and does not allow for procrastination during the day

Closeout items. Stop saying, *I will finish this tomorrow* as this statement will continue to roll work over for longer than it needs to. When planning your day, focus on fitting in enough tasks to fill it rather than overflow it. This has helped me to switch off once I have logged off rather than think about what I did not complete during the day.

Plan for after work. Let's be honest, when you work from home the day can drag. Planning to see friends, catch a gym class or read that book you have been thinking about can motivate you to be productive throughout the day to reward yourself at the end. This has also helped me to reset for the next day by putting me in a positive mindset to attack the workload ahead.

Summary

As a young professional, it is not always the technical skills you learn that set you apart but rather the softer skills that many tend to overlook. As more young people are starting their careers working from home, they may not have the same opportunity to get into good working habits and I hope this article has helped you in some way to get some good habits and be more productive. Having a flexible personality where you can manage your time and subsequently, productivity levels will be held in much higher regard than someone who has learnt to operate an IT system or can reel off a product suite to a customer. So, take advantage of this time as the early growth in your personal development under these working conditions can be outstanding.

About Safa Arif

Over the last five years, Safa Arif has worked for some great brands across Europe including Bosch and United Carpets. She is currently a Business Analyst at NatWest, which is part of the RBS Group.

Her specific interests are in Business, Entrepreneurship and Finance and she loves to learn about these topics through the amazing tools available in this digital age. She would love to connect with organisations and professionals who share this journey.

She has written a number of articles that have been published online and also did a series of radio interviews commenting on the BBC Apprentice show recently.

Connect with Safa:

Linkedin.com/in/safaarif

Twitter.com/SafaArif2

The Challenge of Leadership Managing A Team When Everyone Is Working From Home

Adesola Orimalade

Remote Working or *Working from Home* is a practice that has been adopted by many organisations worldwide. Although it has its' critics, over the last few years many organisations, keen to tempt the younger generation had started to offer *Working from Home* as one of the *benefits* offered to employees.

As someone who has had the privilege of working for some of the largest corporate organisations including the Royal Bank of Scotland, John Lewis Partnership and Bank of America I understand the *Why* and *How Working from Home* can be made to be operationally viable.

In these organisations I have also managed teams of various sizes and my direct reports; due to various reasons, have had to work from home. In some cases, these organisations, especially those within financial services have a structure that allows the BCP (Business Continuity Plans) to be tested at least once a year. The rule was always around 80/20 i.e. 80% working from home and 20% working in some form of office environment, usually in a separate location.

It would be safe for me to say therefore that prior to March 2020, I had experience of:

- Managing a team in situ with the ability to have physical contact with my team members and
- Remotely managing a team where I was based in one location and the rest of the team were based in one location offshore.
- Managing a team under a BCP test scenario where some members of the team worked from home or from the office and a few select team members (deemed in critical roles) work from a separate location
- Managing a team where from time to time, members of my team will request to work from home usually to meet personal needs. These were usually for short length of time.

In March 2020 however, the world as we know it changed significantly. The Covid-19 pandemic has moved from simply being an outbreak in Asia to a global pandemic sweeping across international borders. In a bid to stem the tide of infection, countries and organisations pushed for *Social Distancing* and as a consequence, it became immediately obvious that where possible organisations were going to be requesting employees to work remotely and from home.

When my current employers decided therefore that all members of staff were to work from home, it was to become an entirely new experience for me and a test of my leadership competencies.

The last few weeks have been both eye opening and provided me with a platform to developing other skills and competencies.

When you are managing a team remotely the first challenge is ensuring that everyone has the hardware and software system to work from home.

The recent experience with Covid-19 has shown that all

organisations need to have a robust BCP plan that is tried and tested.

The second challenge I discovered was that I needed to set targets and expectations but also allow team members the leeway to use their initiatives

Trust is a critical ingredient.

There are a few key items I have found to be quite useful in managing teams and showing leadership whilst working from home during periods of serious global event as the Covid-19 pandemic of 2020.

Be Focussed On People

It is important to note that despite all the pros that is attributed to *Working from Home*, it is equally important to highlight that remote working is not ideal for everyone. I have met people in my career who find leaving their residence and going to a separate location for work is therapeutic, it gives a sense of purpose.

The leader should check on the mental and physical wellbeing of team members. There are tangible steps that are recommended and these would include

- Allowing team members, a safe place where they can ventilate any issues that they may have with the home working environment
- You as leader need to be reassuring that it is in order for team members to have children wander into view whilst there is a conference call
- Encourage frequent breaks from their work station

Set Clear Goals And Targets But Avoid The Urge To Micro-Manage

Good leadership, involves giving direction while also developing direct and indirect reports. In some cases, it can feel like there are more deliverables when all team members are working from home. It is just an illusion and in my view that is a feeling that comes because as a leader the ability to see tasks being initiated and completed is greatly reduced. You have to rely on trust that the work is being done.

The alternative would be to ask to be copied on all correspondence which again is not healthy in the long run.

It is important therefore to identify that when remote working being clear on deliverables is even more important. As a leader understanding the composition of your team in terms of:

- Who would need the most support and hand holding maybe due to the fact that they are the newest members of the team?
- Who is/re more independent in terms of experience and can self-motivate and self-manage?
- Where is the most operational risk and how can that be best managed

Have Minimum One Virtual Meeting A Day

The availability of tools such as Skype and Zoom means that you don't necessarily need to be a technical whizz-kid to be able to arrange, organise and lead virtual huddles and meetings.

These meetings are important not just to discuss targets, address customer, service or product issues but should be run in a manner that there is room for team members to interact. In many cases and subject to the culture of the organisation and team, allowing conversation around other issues that are occurring outside work should be allowed.

At the end of the day the huddle is formal and informal. In an ideal situation, co-workers get time to meet and talk face to face and the huddle is an opportunity to encourage engagement with each other.

Recognise The Multi-Cultural Nature Of Your Organisation And Team

There is additional consideration to bear in mind if all or part of your team are globally dispersed. It is important to understand that culture and tradition do tend to influence how people work and relate at home.

A good example is a situation where a team member based in another country was uncomfortable with activating the video option for a conference call, due to cultural and religious consideration.

What may be acceptable or the norm in terms of conduct whilst working from home for one person may have a different connotation to another team member based on cultural and religious norms acceptable in the two countries.

Emotional Intelligence Is A Valuable Leadership Skill

One of the key risks of remote working especially when interwoven with external influences such as home worker acting as a carer to relatives or with restricted movement as is the case during a pandemic, isolation can have a negative effect on performance. Be aware and be mindful of the impact of these on team members.

In an ideal scenario you, as a team leader, should arrange and encourage opportunities for those remote working and those who work in "brick and mortar" locations to meet as frequently as possible. There are organisations for example that organise yearly events such as conferences or seminars where all team members are expected to attend.

Where the opportunity to have these types of face to face meetings is limited by funs or other external factors, the team lead should encourage team members to use various tools to correspond.

Get team members to ask themselves:

- Why am I using emails only to interact with other team members?
- Can I pick up the phone and call?
- What about using Instant Messaging instead of emails?

These other modes of contract can be more personal than emails and also break the monotony that constant stream of email correspondence for a prolonged period can have.

The final point to note is that many good leaders tend to focus a lot of energy in making sure that their team members are well looked after especially when they are working from home.

As laudable as those qualities are, it is important t for you as a leader not to neglect your own mental health and wellbeing.

Working from Home has its pros and cons and it can place additional pressure on leadership. Taking time off to reflect and re-energise is important so you can continue to add value to the team.

About Adesola Orimalade

Adesola Orimalade is an experienced Treasury, Trade Finance, Credit and Transactional Finance Manager who has managed teams of various sizes working for organisations including Standard Chartered Bank, Royal Bank of Scotland, John Lewis Partnership, Hogg Robinson Partnership, Bank of America and Orsted Limited.

He supports four UK charities including as Chair of the Board of Trustees for Citizens' Advice Redbridge, Motivational Speaker for Working Options in Education, Mentor for Migrant Leaders and Business Trainer for Consonant (formerly Migrant Resource Centre).

In addition, he is passionate about developing people and in his spare time he enjoys running workshops and seminars in the UK including a recent Workshop titled *Day In The Life Of A Transactional Finance Manager* delivered to postgraduate students of the Nottingham University Business School.

A writer and playwright, his work has been featured by magazines including The Finance Director, Real Leaders and the Globalist.

www.linkedin.com/in/adesola-harold-orimalade

Juggling The Balls Of Parenting, Your Brand And Working From Home

Jo Baldwin Trott

The working from home tribe has grown exponentially almost overnight. You may be revelling in the fact that you no longer have to go to work, or you may be finding it a huge challenge. Whichever camp you fit into or if you are somewhere in between the guarantee is that you will find it a challenge working from home with the family around.

This chapter delves into how you can lead from your sofa ensuring your brand is nurtured as well as your kids. How you can retain your productivity, energy and sanity whilst juggling a family. What starts off as an exciting novelty can wear off pretty quickly if you unless you consider these key factors.

I've been remote working for nine years and still find it challenging however, I have identified four key areas which need strategic thinking to make your job a whole lot easier: remote awareness; boundary setting; environment; communication.

Mindful Remoteness

The very first thing to do is to stop and acknowledge what you are doing. This may sound obvious but it is so easy to go into top speed and continue where you left off when you last left the office. It is key that as humans, we allow ourselves to be fully present in the challenges we are facing. By pausing and recognising that life has changed in a very big way and that you are now a manager/employee/entrepreneur and also a full time parent, you will begin to value the challenge. By giving yourself frequent breaks throughout the day you are not only resetting your body and posture you are checking in with your processing. We are all processing so much right now, give yourself time to do so and talk it over with your family.

Boundaries And Knowing When To Stop

I remember the day I decided to work from home and launch a business. I was a mixture of petrified, relieved, excited, inspired and a little bit smug. After various careers in policing, customer service, sales and teaching I had had my fare share of *painfully slow commuting into a large city. Bristol was proudly awarded the worst city to drive around for a very good reason.

I was sick of weekend working, as a teacher and police officer and I have never been very good at being told what to do. I had also separated from my husband so self-employment meant flexibility. Becoming the boss meant I could make up the rules. But I forgot to.

The first lesson I have learnt is to define your boundaries. Most of my clients at the start were women and mothers so within a very short time I was once again working many evenings, weekends, too and although my income was hitting my targets my lack of boundaries was impacting my quality time with my family, and myself. Your work/business should be just that. If it becomes a beast – it runs you, terrifies you and governs you – or a baby – you can't put it down, you want to nurture it 24/7 – then you need to change the rules.

It is vital that working from home with a family you create a routine with strict timings and right now routine is helping people to cope. As humans we like routine and setting in stone a structure to your days leads to productive relationships with yourself, your family and your business. Without structure you run the very high risk of neglecting one or more of those relationships.

Create a structure and let everyone know. I would also recommend everyone has a timetable in these times of lockdown, it allows us to achieve and progress. I have a clear routine which is simple, allows time for me, my business and my family and simply helps me to stay sane...

My Day

07:00 – 07:30 - MEDITATION

07:30 – 07:45 - YOGA

07:45 – 08:15 – EXERCISE (HIIP TRAINING)

08:15 – 09:00 – BREAKFAST

09:00 – 10:00 – WORK SESSION 1 – EMAILS AND COMMUNICATION

10:00 – 13:00 – WORK SESSION 2 – CREATIVE TIME/WRITING/ VIDEO CONTENT

13:00 – 17:00 – WORK WITH CLIENTS

17:00 - WORKING DAY ENDS

Create your own timetable or set timings in your phone. Use your online or paper diary but set reminders on your phone for starting work, finishing work, breaks and finishing work. That's not a typo. Just because you can doesn't mean you should and just because you can work an extra hour to just get this __________ done it doesn't mean you should.

Even as I write this I am mindful of the fact that I am heading into overtime but it is a rare thing for me, normally 5 pm. I am done. Especially as a team leader, it is likely you will be encouraging your staff to finish on time to ensure they have quality time with the family. You need to too, and you also need to be a role model for how to make remote working work.

Environment

Probably one of the biggest challenges of remote working is creating an optimal working environment. Some of you will have or feel you need an office with a door to remove yourself from the mayhem of family life. Personally, that's not my thing and I have two working zones in the house – my kitchen table (creative writing/admin/collaborator video calls) and my lounge (all professional video/interviews for my TV show/client calls). I tried the shut in my office approach but I like to feel connected with people and work better from my kitchen table than I do a closed off room. I love to work in cafe's but that, like everything, is on pause right now.

Whichever you feel is right for you commit to making it work. But there are a few questions you need to ask yourself to create a productive work zone:

- What exactly do I need to do from that zone?
- Will I be distracted/interrupted?
- Will I be working to my best potential?
- Is it sustainable for my work and my body?

If all requirements aren't met for each of those purposes then you are setting yourself up to fail. Your zone needs to support your body in a healthy and comfortable way and allow for your work practise. It must create the right impression for your brand but also encourage you to focus.

Showing Up On Video

Video creates instant impact with your customers and clients. We are all on video. Our technology allows us to communicate globally and with hundreds at a time through video conferencing. But not giving your visual environment enough attention is brand damage, lack of faith from your clients or customers. Even a de-valued team.

Every time you engage with a colleague or client on either the telephone or on a video call you are communicating our brand and our values. By answering the phone with the washing machine on in the background, even if you reassure your caller that the spin cycle is about to finish and the helicopter in their ear will stop it is distracting and worse, unprofessional. Taking calls in a quiet room with no noise is best, always.

When it comes to video calls the details really matter.

I have had so many calls with clients who are coaches, who work entirely remotely and offer exceptional quality and skills. And yet when I go online for a video call they have failed to value the importance of what I see. They show up with notes on the wall, a messy study, bad lighting and it damages their credential.

I am writing a whole book on the energy of who we are, and what we see. The importance of how you show up as your brand should never be overlooked, but to summarise: everything you see you judge; everything you see sends a message; everything you see tells a story; everything you see tells us something about your brand. Declutter, simplify, and ensure that everything your caller sees fits in with your brand as much as possible. Your animalistic nature tells you to judge, you are designed to, you can't help it. Go to my video on YouTube channel for my *How to show up on video calls - https://youtu.be/6puuKeLTYQI*

Make sure the lighting is bright. Your caller is seeing a picture, if you're in shadow they can't see you properly.

What you wear really matters and the latest statistics tell us that we are judged by what we wear and how we look in less than a second. It is vital that remote workers recognise the importance of dressing up for the occasion, getting out of your tracksuit /comfy trousers unless it is congruent to your brand. The key word here is consistency.

If you have decided to go casual for a call and are wearing a t-shirt rather than your usual shirt and jacket, your caller will instantly make decisions on the fact that you are casual, that you aren't in your normal business clothes and they may feel that you are not being business-like. If you normally live and breath in gym gear for work then continue to do so but it is important to maintain standards and reassure your clients and colleagues that business is continuing. As is your efficiency and professionalism.

I have worked with women speakers that purposefully and unusually wear heeled shoes on stage as it gives them a different feeling, makes them more aware of their body, body language and posture. It triggers them to be on the top of their game.

To be our best we need to feel our best and that means wearing the right clothes that create those feelings, it also helps us to flip into business/work mode and out of mum/dad mode.

Wear colour. The colour black suits very few skin tones, and for most cultures suggests solemnity and strong authority, is that your brand message? Even my friend and funeral celebrant Benn Abdy-Collins never wears black, unless he has to. Navy flatters all, but bright is best and the vibration of colour lifts us instantly. Another book.

We all look better in colour and can all wear bright colours. I recommend investing in an online colour analysis and image review. Do the most you can to give the right impression. I, and many Image experts offer online consultations.

Show up and be seen to be remembered.

Give yourself 15 minutes before your call to check the camera is at eye level, your technology is working and that your kids know it's do not disturb time.

Communication - Recruiting Your Family

Communicating with your children and/or partner is key to a positive remote working environment. My kids know to leave me alone first thing in the morning as I'm meditating. Thankfully they are old enough to be self-sufficient. When they were younger I got up an hour earlier than them to make sure I meditated and had my Me Time. This was a game-changer for me and I can't recommend it enough, the first few minutes of your day should be about you, in peace and gratitude.

Tell your kids/partner what you're doing that day, keep them informed. Tell them you have an important call with a really good customer. Bring them into the picture and allow them to be part of your remote working journey. Get them to make a Do not disturb sign for your door. Let them be your human resource and personnel department. Give them a badge! They will love to feel connected to your work and the more they know, the more chance they will appreciate what you do and will be happy to leave you to it.

The Joy Of Being Home As A Parent

I recommend you begin the journey with a focus on pragmatism not perfection. Remote working can be a bumpy ride: just watch Professor Robert Kelly's interview on YouTube.

Distractions are a given. But with the right preparation and boundary setting they can be managed. If you have ever watched Oprah live on TV you will have seen how polished and perfect her TV shows are. Amidst COVID19, Oprah is now interviewing from her size of my ground floor study, and is online like the rest of us. But it doesn't always go to plan. Technology and toddler glitches happen.

Seeing yourself as having three relationships – with yourself, your family, and your business - is fundamental to successful remote working. This allows you to create an efficient stress free working environment that leverages your brand. You will begin to enjoy it and feel good which is always the best way of working.

During these challenging times we are all creating new work practices and new ways of existing. If you can make a success of remote working now, then it's likely you can build on that success. Right know if feels like we are all shifting the focus back onto the family and lifestyle, the most important parts of our life.

After a decade of remote working as a parent I have at last nailed it and I love it. My children are now older, so it is much easier for them to understand how I need to work. They've also become adaptable, independent and supportive. I'm really proud of them.

My puppy, however, is still in training. Welcome to my world.

[1] Galinsky, A. & Hajo, A. (2012) Journal of Experimental Psychology, Volume 48, Issue 4.

About Jo Baldwin Trott

Jo Baldwin Trott mentors established SMEs, executives, leaders, politicians, personalities - typically professionals in highly visible roles. She specialises in personal branding, with an emphasis on what she calls *the energy of showing up*.

Profiled clients include leading fertility expert Dr. Ashish Paul; TV celebrity Martin Roberts and legend, Eddie 'The Eagle' Edwards.

Jo is a lecturer at the London College of Style; a member of the Professional Speakers Association and director for gender equality group 50:50 Parliament.

Jo is an author in *Remote Working* and her forthcoming book, *The Energy Of Showing Up* will be released this summer available for pre-order at *www.jobaldwintrott.com/products*

She is a golfer, sings in a band and loves road tripping with her kids in California.

Check out *Jo's Amijo Show* live on Zoom at 2pm
or on YouTube *https://youtu.be/qHZTQk95rDY*

Connect on LinkedIn *www.linkedin.com/in/jobaldwintrott*

Follow her on Instagram:
https://www.instagram.com/jobaldwintrott/

Tweet at

https://mobile.twitter.com/Jobaldwintrott

Or go to her website:

www.jobaldwintrott.com

Six Simple Ideas For More Effective Home Working

Nick Meinertzhagen

Recently there have been huge increases in the number of people working from home. Effective home working isn't easy, it doesn't happen by luck or by chance. You need to plan and set yourself up to succeed.

I founded my first business from my spare bedroom back in 2004 and worked there for over two years before moving into rented office space. I significantly grew the company and sold my business in 2018. Now I find myself working from home again - but not much has changed. Whilst technology makes things much easier than it used to, the core techniques I used for effective home working are still just as valid today.

I have highlighted six simple ideas (in no particular order) which I would like to share with you.

1. Structure Your Working Day (And Stick To It)

Break down your working day into structured segments. Know when you want to start work at your desk and when you want to finish your day. To others in the household it may seem strange that at 08:55 you are focused on needing to *get to work* – even if that is going to your office in the spare room. Build in time for lunch and breaks away from your desk as these will keep you fresh, energised and focused on what you need to do, which will ultimately make your day more productive. In every job there are tasks that you won't enjoy as much as others, so I recommend planning these lower interest tasks before your favoured ones. This means you won't procrastinate as much; you will get the mundane tasks done quicker thus allowing you to move onto the more enjoyable tasks. Creating a working structure is really important, but you have to be disciplined and stick to it.

2. Set Written Milestones (And Reflect On Your Achievements)

Within your working day, it is important to set focused milestones of what you aim to achieve. Milestones are stages you would like to reach in a project or alternatively tasks that you may want to fully complete. I suggest breaking each day's target achievements into segments, for example, *I am aiming to get tasks a, b and c finished by my morning break*. Doing this will help you remain focused, keep you motivated and not overwhelmed. I advise you to write down each element of what you want to achieve and when completed you tick them off your whiteboard, cross them off your paper task list or do whatever gives you a sense of immediate achievement. At the end of each day reflect on what you have achieved, as this is particularly important when working at home because often there is no-one else to pat you on the back or to say well done.

3. Avoid Temptations And Chores (And Do Them Earlier, Or Later)

Working from home is a difficult environment as you are constantly surrounded by reminders. This might be a temptation of something nice, or the never-ending list of mundane chores you have to do. Irrespective of what these are you need to be disciplined and do them outside of your working day. Small tasks such as putting the washing on or loading the dishwasher – may seem like quick little jobs, but added together can consume important time plus they keep switching your mindset away from your work. Often doing these jobs leads to a vicious circle of other small jobs or to inter-related jobs (i.e. hanging out the washing, unloading the dishwasher, etc). In reality, it is not easy to ignore these things and it takes a huge amount of self-discipline to say that *worktime is for work.* If there are chores then why not see if you can get a few done before you start the day, and if there is something tempting that you want to do, then why not make that your own reward for your day's achievement.

4. Stay Connected (And Learn Something New)

When working at home it is important to purposely build in time for human-to-human contact, so endeavour to make time every day to stay connected. As human beings we are designed to interact with other people, so if feasible, you could start your day with a call to a colleague or by contacting a customer, etc. Think if you can switch from a phone call to a video call, as this makes your whole engagement richer. Also, during your interactions with customers, colleagues or suppliers, don't just make conversations about work – why not try to learn more about the people you are speaking with. Try and learn something new each time you engage with someone, such as their interests, their family, what they did last night, etc. This will not only forge more meaningful and longer lasting relationships, but it will also make your working day more enriching for you.

5. Create Your Working Area (And Keep The Boundaries Separate)

Living and working in the same environment can be very pressured, so where possible try and create a designated working area. Whilst I appreciate that this is not always possible, you might be able to be creative in how you achieve this in your own home environment. When no boundaries exist, it is easy for your work and your homelife to become intertwined. Working and living in close proximity makes it easy to slip into doing little bits of work outside of your core working day. Also try to avoid the temptation of accessing your work emails outside of your day and remember if it can wait till your next working day, then make it wait. You need to consciously remind yourself to maintain these home/work boundaries, as things can very quickly and easily become blurred - which is not in anyone's best interests.

6. Engage Your Family (And Your Work Colleagues)

No home living situations are identical and there is no *one size fits all* to home working. It is important to engage the people in your household about how you intend to work and how they can support you. If your household are not understanding or empathetic to what you need to do then it may cause personal conflicts. Having a structure and rules work well, especially where there are children in the household. Very quickly children learn these rules and they will become the new normal. Remember, although you are working from home that doesn't mean you can't reach out to other friends or colleagues for mutual support and guidance. You could share what works well, things that have not worked well and together you will all be stronger.

Hopefully, I have given you some inspiration or simply some reassurance that you are doing the right things. Remember, working from home is not easy, so take some time to understand the blend of your own home situation, demands of your work structure, your strengths and weaknesses. Then you can create an effective home working plan which is just right for you.

About Nick Meinertzhagen

Nick Meinertzhagen (MBA) is a Customer Strategist and Entrepreneur. He founded one of the UK's largest covert customer measurement businesses, which he sold in 2018. Nick now runs his own strategic consultancy.

www.ExperientialConsulting.co.uk

https://www.linkedin.com/in/meinertzhagen/

Your Mind Will Determine Your Success – Use It Wisely

Penny Power

It took a mental shock for me to respect my mind. I abused it for twenty-two years, showed it no respect and expected so much of it. Then, one day it said enough!

I was a *remote worker,* an entrepreneur and one day, I questioned it all. My words here follow my journey to deep happiness and fulfilment. You've picked up this book because the cover resonates with you; my intention is to share with you the importance of your mind and how to manage adversity when you are remote and sometimes feel alone.

In November 2018, I was diagnosed with PTSD and a form of depression called *The Curse of the Strong'* a condition named by Psychiatrist Dr Tim Cantopher and a book available to buy on Amazon.

What I discovered at that moment of mental dis-ease, and in the following beautiful ten months of therapy, was that I had an incredible level of mental strength, but an appalling level of mental fitness. I never set boundaries, I never meditated or walked just for pleasure and I never considered my own needs. I had become a machine, albeit, I was loving and caring, but never to myself. I was a busy fool, in more ways than one.

Since that period of repair and discovery, my sense of balance, contentment, creativity, joy, happiness and success has been greater than at any other time in my life. I sustain it, I honour it and I will never mis-treat myself or allow others to again. Upon reflection, I had been unknowingly self-abusing.

Since publishing my book, *Business is Personal* and since deeply supporting other entrepreneurs and remote workers, I have now learned that many others are similar to the way I was. Few of us look after our minds.

Looking back on the past 10 years, I have been through 11 moments of trauma. Major body blows which individually, should have made me step back and take time to recover. They were financial, life changing phone calls that took the rug out from under us. They were emotional shocks of the death of loved ones, family members who were too young to die; and one was a huge traumatic event within our family.

All 11 traumas required strength and adaptability, life had to change for us. Last year, my daughter and I spoke at a TedX Talk called, *Do you need adversity to find true happiness?*, I believe you do. There is growth in adversity; I have learned to trust it and believe in it and know that happiness will return.

Throughout all of these events, putting oxygen on others and caring for those around me was my priority. I know this is not unique, we all do this. This is why the words *in the event of oxygen failing on a plane, put your mask on first*, is re-quoted so many times. In reality, we rarely do this when we go through major oxygen removing experiences ourselves.

So, what takes away our oxygen?

Shock. It is shock that rocks us to the core and leaves us unable to think clearly. It is physical. The adrenalin and cortisol that enters our body causes our stomachs to ache and cripples our heads. I have discovered that I am now able to predict how I will handle bad news and life-changing moments. I want to share them with you.

For me, I go through each stage rapidly, literally, each step takes a day. However, when I first started to experience lifechanging shocks, this process took months. Over time, I have cut it down, as the fastest I can get to stage four, the fastest I can feel back in control. I hasten to add, none of this has been proven by psychologists, I have proved it only to myself.

Stage 1. The BIG blow.

The moment I am told something that I know will alter my planned course in life, totally out of my control. I know this will require me to access inner strength, trust, belief and creativity to get me through.

It feels like a shot to the stomach. I need to sit with this, carry out some first aid on myself and those that have been affected around me. I need to be very tactical and practical and give myself time to absorb the information. Now is not the time to find solutions and to be strategic or creative.

Stage 2. The Emotions Flow.

I wake very low; I feel all emotions. Fear, anger, sadness, bitterness, regret, grief, the sense of loss. The mountain I was climbing is now disappearing from under my feet. I had felt so prepared for this climb, I had reached Base Camp, and was now enjoying the view. I was feeling a sense of safety here, yet now, despite gripping so tightly to cling on, I was slipping down, seeing the summit of my goals and plans disappear further into the distance. Fear was gripping me, terrified that I will fall badly and will never get back on my path again.

I cry, the disappointment is enormous, I want to blame some-one or something. I lose faith that I can ever do it again, that this mountain and the path I was on, was the only right one.

By night, I am exhausted. All emotions have flooded through my body, and somehow, I feel a sense of acceptance, a realisation that things are different, and I cannot control this. I start to think 'what next? What can I do that is within my control?'.

Stage 3. My Mind Is Fuelled By Something Greater Than Fear.

Having allowed my emotions to flow, my mind is now ready to be clever. Accepting that I have no control over what has happened, I let go of it. I send my past plans and life routines away with love. I make space for my new way of life.

You see, this is the stage when I am truly alive. Confronting my greatest asset and value, the power of love, and empowering myself to use it in this time of need.

I am amazed how connected our heads and hearts are. If I drive my mind with my heart, then I am more powerful than I could ever believe. When I allow my heart to drive me instead of my head, it's like the sun is entering my body. The warmth it gives me is extraordinary. It fills me with the trust, faith and hope that I need to calm my mind, to still my fears and to allow me to be creative and find the solutions I need.

Stage 4. Happiness Returns

Today I wake with such joy, a smile, laughter, I want to listen to music, I want to dance a bit. I want to connect with others, I want to sooth others who might also be in shock or affected by the news I am dealing with. I get excited about the new possibilities and I feel so alive.

My energy has returned and with that comes creativity. I almost thank the world for allowing me to show myself once again *who I am*, as this is far more impactful than *what I am*. No one needs the *what* I was, or could have been, everyone needs the hearts and souls of others to heal, to connect and to find shared ways to move forward. Life is now moving forward. I can do this, I am ready.

I share these stages in the total awareness that you might be experiencing one of them now, and if not now, then you will be one day. Adversity is a human experience that we all have. This is never your own battle. We each have battles, large and small, every day. Surviving pain and change is a human journey.

The challenge for many of us, is that when you work remotely, you are in danger of thinking you are alone, that your battle is unique and that the world *has it in for you.*

This is why we must all unite and leave behind our fake identities and fake communication. We need to be the beacons of real life and connect in communities that reflect and honour this.

However, this is not easy. People hide their truth behind their identity. This is the mission I have in life: to help others to be themselves and allow their own battles to be shared, to have confidence and to love the real you.

Since Thomas and I founded Ecademy in 1998, we have seen the energy and power of real people. You can choose how you want to filter the world; I choose to filter the real, from the fake and the loving people from the ego driven people. We can surround ourselves with the right people, we just need to know who we are seeking.

My words to you are with love. I want to finish by saying: love yourself deeply, it is not wrong to do this and give yourself space and time to regain control when you have challenges thrown at you.

You are the greatest asset in your business and career, treat yourself this way and you will find your way to your definition of success and happiness. As I state in my book and every day to myself, *What is the life you want to lead?*; it is within your control and your head and your heart can take you there.

About Penny Power

Penny was Awarded her OBE 2014 for her *contribution to entrepreneurs in the Digital Economy,* citing the work her and her husband, Thomas, did to bring Social Networking to Small Business in 1998 before anyone else in the world did. Working with Business Owners has been their life ever since.

Penny and Thomas now run a unique Mastermind Program that allows the members to build their businesses into the type of business and life they have always wanted. Considering their personal skills and choices in life. Penny's latest book *Business is Personal* is helping thousands of business owners to find their success and happiness in business.

www.pennypower.co.uk/businesshealthcheck

Twitter @pennypower

Insta @pennyfpower

The Future Of Work

Michael Davis-Marks

Introduction

The world of work is changing. Long before the Coronavirus pandemic inflicted a massive blight on the health and normal daily routines of billions of citizens' lives, or the potential impact on the global economy, the exponential growth of digital connectivity, mobile devices and information is driving profound changes in the way we work, all around the world. Known in some circles as the *Future of Work*, thought leaders in this space imagined a world in which people added value in different ways to today and the ability to work more flexibly, both in time and geographically was the principal driver.

Not everyone, however, shares this 'Utopian' dream and the impact of IoT/AI on jobs was and is being hotly debated. Notwithstanding this, the fact remains that technology gives a significant proportion of us more options in how we choose to work, as evidenced by the rapid increase in home/remote working over the last ten years. In fact, when you are able to work from anywhere, why go to the office? Yes, human (face to face) connections matter, but needn't be the sole driver of productivity and increasingly aren't.

Impact Of Covid-19

The actions by many nation states and the fears of millions of individuals as a result of the widespread outbreak of the coronavirus in early 2020 has caused many people to be forced to work from home. For those of us who have chosen to work from home before the pandemic struck (in my case for the last 7 years), this is not such a significant change as we have adapted tools and techniques allowing us to contribute just as effectively, if not more so to the world of work, than we did beforehand. But for the majority, this will be a strange environment and whilst some will take to the extraordinary and rapid change in circumstances like a *duck to water*, it is likely that many will need help and guidance to maximise the chances of success in the 'remote workplace'.

This article seeks to help those people currently adapting to working from home.

Routines

First things first. It is very tempting when working from home to work as and when you feel like it. From experience, I know that it becomes very easy to procrastinate (more than usual) and be distracted by some jobs that need doing around the house or by other people in the house, perhaps not working in the same way. With home working, it is really important to set boundaries - not rigid ones that can never be broken, but a set of rules that you and others in the house agree to abide to most of the time. Here are some top tips for setting routines:

- **Get changed.** However tempting it is to *go to work* in your pyjamas, from a mindset perspective, it is really important that you make the effort to change into *work* clothes. That does not mean that, if you normally work in a suit or uniform (for example), that you should wear these at home, but the routine of getting up, showering, dressing for work, having breakfast and brushing your teeth, is important in preparing your mindset for work. Of course this activity might well be done later than usual to factor in the lack of commuting to work and may for some people be a welcome bonus, but this will be on a case by case basis. Some people function best first thing in the morning, whilst others (me included) are better a little later in the day. It's *horses for courses* and you will know what works for you best.

- **Create a place to work.** You may already have a home office or study, even if you are not used to working from home, but if you don't, it is really important to establish somewhere to work that is free from the noises and other distractions of the house. If you are lucky to have a spare bedroom or a dining room that doesn't get routinely used, establish this as your new office and make sure other occupants of the house understand and agree with this. Once this is established, limit work related paraphernalia to this space and don't encroach on other parts of the house. Apart from being considerate to other members of the family, it also helps your concentration and efficiency if it's all in one place.
- **Stay Active.** Actually, this applies just as much to working in an office, but the science is starting to show that sitting down all day is bad for your health and restricts creativity if you don't change your *scenery* every so often. Evidence suggests that in sedimentary jobs, it is advisable and beneficial to stand up and stretch your legs every 30 mins. And whilst current government instructions (at the time of writing) are to *Stay at Home* you are allowed out once a day for a period of exercise and it is good practice to just pop out of your *office* every now and again for a change of scenery.
- **Keep in touch.** One of the early observations about home working is the lack of social activity - the inability to have a quick chat with a work colleague or to gather around the water cooler (if you have one at work) to chat about life, work and play. But I have found that it is just as easy to have a quick chat via the many virtual ways of doing so, via video if you so choose (that's another reason why it's important to get dressed) and once you get used to calling someone in the same way as you might pop your head round the door in the office, it will quickly become second nature. I find it is courteous to message them first with a quick *u free?* to avoid bothering them during a (virtual) meeting or another call.

- **Switch off.** It may sound obvious, but if you are working from home, it is also important to switch off from work at the end of the work day. Normally, the act of commuting or going to the gym after work does this for us, but it is important for you AND the other people you are living with to separate work from the other parts of your life. So when you leave the area or room you have designated as your *workspace* leave your work and thoughts about work in the room.

Connectivity

One of the most important things in working from home is being able to connect with your work colleagues and clients/customers. Technology and innovation have provided a smorgasbord of choice in terms of systems, but all require, at the very least, a good and reliable broadband connection. If you are lucky enough to have fibre optic superfast broadband in your area, that is a great advantage, so those working in rural areas might face some challenges here, but the golden rule is get the best you can get (which doesn't necessarily mean paying a lot). I find that consumer advisory groups like Which? are a good source for information on what's best for you.

Assuming you have got a decent level of connectivity, you should now look at how you communicate with other people connected to your work. Here are some other things to consider:

- **Use collaborative rather than binary tools.** When email first arrived on the scene, we all marvelled at the ability to push out information and gather feedback at the speed of light. Your 'normal' office may not be set up for this, but it would be helpful if internal communications could be conducted on a team platform like Slack, Podio or Microsoft Teams (other platforms are available). The benefits of working in a collaborative way that creates discussions and consultations in the same way as we speak to each other is vastly superior to an email thread which suffers from the 'Reply All' syndrome and soon gets lost.

- **Use the Cloud.** In the same way, passing round documents and inviting comments or track changes is much harder work and less collaborative than using a cloud based document system like Google Drive, iCloud or Office 365. It avoids multiple versions and duplicate documents and allows anyone in the team invited to view, comment or edit the latest version even to the point of 'live editing'. Best of all, it is accessible from multiple devices meaning that when you are out and about (when that's allowed), you can access it on your phone or laptop.
- **Share Calendars.** If you are set up to use the collaborative tools in the first two points above, the next natural progression is to share your calendars with everyone in your team on the same cloud based platform. The benefit this has is in the ability to look to see if someone else is free to talk before contacting them or arranging impromptu or ad hoc meetings quickly. Just because you are working from home doesn't mean you can't tell if they are 'in the office' or not.

Conclusions

Even before Covid-19 struck the planet, the ability to work in a more flexible way from wherever you wanted was starting to attract converts. Enlightened organisations already intent on decentralising decision making and empowering their people with information have seen significantly better employee engagement as a result and are drivers for further change. And as the world becomes more interconnected, value creation is shifting from the individual to the collective.

With large numbers of people now confined to working from home to avoid spreading the virus, technology is allowing us to work more collectively and collaboratively, wherever we may be. Whilst this article has been written to help those trying to adapt to home working for, perhaps, the first time, it also recognises that in the future, this way of working might become the norm.

The Future of Work is here.

About Mike Davis-Marks OBE

Mike Davis-Marks (MDM) enjoyed a 36 year career in the Royal Navy, having wanted to join the Service since the age of seven. During that time, he served in a wide variety of leadership roles in both submarines and surface ships, culminating in a testing three year command of the hunter killer nuclear powered submarine, HMS TURBULENT. He has also navigated a submarine to the North Pole (twice), taught Officer Cadets leadership at Britannia Royal Naval College, held a diplomatic post at the British Embassy in Washington DC (during the period of 9/11) and was awarded the OBE for his part in planning and running the International Fleet Review in 2005.

Since leaving the Navy in 2013, he joined a group of Social Entrepreneurs, who are looking at how technology and innovation can be used to drive collaborations into solving complex social and environmental problems and are also experimenting on the Future of Work.

He is currently the Director of Building Pathways Ltd, providing pre-employment mentoring and training for marginalised people as well as a leadership facilitator and coach with the True Leader Company. MDM qualified as a NLP practitioner in 2012 and believes that people are a company's most important asset and that investing in your workforce will deliver much greater dividends than merely trying to maximise shareholder profit.

Web: buildingpathways.org.uk

LI: https://www.linkedin.com/in/mike-davis-marks-081b4212/

Twitter: jollijacktar

A Perspective On Remote Working With A Maslow Twist

Megan Germann

I have been working remotely for nearly a decade now. Focused in data analysis, I've found that a remote environment works well because I can get the quiet that I need to think and concentrate. I am also an introvert; I thrive in keeping to myself and being alone. Don't get me wrong – I loved my time in collaborative office environments where nerf darts flew over my head and there was constant chatter and interaction. But we are in an ever-changing business environment where remote working is becoming more and more prevalent.

Many factors (pandemics, better technology, altered mindset that the right candidate is more important than the location of a candidate, etc.) are changing the face of how businesses work. Remote working is here to stay.

I'd like to give you some advice on what I've found that works in building a rewarding remote career, while at the same time maintaining sanity in solitude. You may be like me and appreciate being remote, or you may be an extrovert who enjoys interaction with others. Regardless, I hope that these tips and tricks I've learned over the years will help make a transition to remote working easier for you.

I like to think of setting yourself up for success working remotely as correlating working needs to Maslow's hierarchy of psychological needs.

Physiological Needs: Find A Place To Work That Works For You

Determine where you are going to get your work done. This does not have to be an established *work area* in your house. Though I have a dedicated office in my home, I tend to move around the house depending on my mood and needs. I'll work at the kitchen table, on the couch, on the porch, or even at a café just to get out. Here are somethings to consider:

- Make sure it's comfortable for you so you can maximize your brain power and get your work done. Establish your work zone where you can easily concentrate.
- Ensure you have all the tools you need for success. Obtain an extra computer monitor, printer, technology to connect to others, etc. This also includes sufficient call and WiFi coverage ... nothing kills productivity like internet outages.
- Be sure to also test the technology where you are. If you are on a video call and your environment doesn't lend itself for you to be connected through computer audio, adjust your inputs or find a new location.
- If you are someone who easily gets distracted, be sure to create a quiet location, free from disruptions.

Safety Needs: Get Up And Move

This isn't safety per-se, but bear with me as I attempt to overlay remote working to Maslow's terminology. Think of *safety* as health. Remote workers tend to be more sedentary than those who go into an office, just by the nature of staying at home. We're not walking from our car into the office, the bathroom is a lot closer, etc.

Get up and move as much as possible to maintain your physical and mental health. Here are some things that work for me:

- Go for a walk, even if it's a short 15 minute walk, during a break.
- Pace or walk in place during (non-video) conference calls.
- Need a bathroom break? Walk to the one furthest from where you are working.
- Wear a fitness tracker to keep you accountable and make sure you get enough steps in.
- Rock some exercise reps or weights during webinars.

Love And Belonging: Work At Communication And Relationships

It's harder to establish relationships with co-workers when working remotely. This is especially true if others are in an office together and you are solo in working separately. It's vital to establish good communication and relationship strategies to maintain effective connections. I focus on each and every one of these daily:

- Don't rely on email as your main method of communication. Too much can get lost in translation. This was a hard one for me to accept. I love email because it's efficient (email sent=an item checked off my to-do list!) and things are in writing. However, people can too easily misread tone and intent, especially if they don't know you personally. For key communication and discussion needs, I started setting up quick chats and then follow-up with a summary email.
- Try to use video conferencing as much as possible. It's much easier to establish connections and relationships when you see someone, even if it's in a virtual capacity. It's also okay to be yourself; no need to dress up. But don't look like you just rolled out of bed. Look presentable.

- Establish some key friendships within your organization. Bonus if they are someone you work with consistently. Get to know them personally, text back and forth ... think of it as a remote water cooler friendship!
- Network within your industry or niche in your town and make in-person connections. Schedule face-to-face lunches, coffees, happy hours, etc.

Esteem: Maintain Your Sense Of Accomplishment

It's easy to feel isolated and uncertain when being remote and away from co-workers. You can lose a sense of how you are doing compared to others and if you are pulling your weight (especially true if you are one of the few remote workers). To maintain a sense of purpose and accomplishment, you should focus on what you will get done that day. I have a very specific method of doing this which I'll outline below. But as with any bit of advice in this book, you have to find what works for you.

- I end each day by making a list of what I'd like to get done the following day. I find that I am more efficient and able to jump right in each morning if the list is already established. Of course, if circumstances have changed from the previous evening, the list can easily be tweaked.
- My list consists of 2 columns; work tasks to do, and personal tasks to do.
- Within each list, I prioritize. What NEEDS to get done today? What can slide to tomorrow? And thirdly, what do I WANT to get done; what will give me the largest sense of accomplishment or satisfaction? On my personal list, I also take into account time to complete a task (can I get it done in 5 minutes between conference calls?).

Self-Actualization: Manage Your Time Efficiently

One of the perks of working from home is the ability to *have more time*. This increase in time is achieved by efficient time management and acknowledging *new time* (i.e., time that is no longer lost to a commute, or time between meetings where not much productive could get done in an office setting). Taking advantage of small pieces of time to get things done will help free up family time, allowing for a much better work-life balance.

- Take 5 minutes between calls to do a quick chore such as throwing in a load of laundry.
- Use your "commute time" to get something (either work related or personal) done; don't waste it by sleeping in.

Final Thoughts

You have to figure out what works for you in your situation. Everyone is different in how they work, so you should have a good idea of what YOU need. Find what makes you happy and makes you work to your best potential. This may change day-to-day, as it does for me, so recognize to what you need that day to work your best and adjust as necessary.

Know your organization. Every company is different in remote working expectations. Learn what is expected of you. Understand the hours you are expected to work. Do you need to be online 8-5? Or do you have flexible hours as long as you get your job done? Also understand what technology you organization uses and make it work to your advantage, especially video conferencing.

It can take some time to master how to maximize your work potential if you are new to remote working. But it's completely achievable by understanding what makes you work most effectively and setting yourself up for success by following some of these tips.

About Megan Germann

Megan Germann is a Certified Customer Experience Professional who has over 15 years of primary and secondary data analysis and market/customer research experience. She has designed and executed Voice of the Customer programs at several Fortune 500 companies in both B2B and B2C capacities.

She is also the founder of her own consulting firm, Megan Germann Insights & Consulting (MGIC) focusing in market/customer research and VoC consulting services.

Megan has been working remotely for nearly a decade, with experience transitioning from an in-office environment to remote working and experience in a fully remote position with team members located globally.

https://www.linkedin.com/in/megan-germann/

Get Paid What You Want, Where You Want

David Rothwell

This article is mostly for people interested in creating a new internet-based business, or taking an existing business and marketing it online, rather than company employees working from home rather than their office (although it may give you ideas and a new side-hustle opportunity too).

New Reality

In today's terrible pandemic, it's tragically ironic for me that remote and home-based working is becoming the new reality for so many people and businesses, when I've been doing it for fifteen years.

So I'm writing this to share with as many people as possible how I was able to use the internet to create an entirely new business which allows me to work where I want, for who I want, and get paid what I ask for from world-wide businesses. Hopefully it will be interesting and above all, useful.

The Reluctant Entrepreneur

On May 27, 2001 I was the Director of European IT for a multinational software company earning £60k pa. The next day I was made redundant in the dotcom crash. After 9/11 later that year Silicon Valley was in meltdown, there were hundreds of people chasing every IT job going, and I was too experienced and too expensive to get another job.

My income had vanished overnight. After more than twenty years in IT, I never worked for another employer except myself. Call me the "Reluctant Entrepreneur"...

Today I am an author, speaker and consultant in the online marketing industry with worldwide clients and associates while working from home and remotely to my own schedule.

House Husband

Along the way I became the house husband, minded children, delivered phone books, got paid to market my own local cleaning business, cleaned houses, cut lawns, did gardening jobs, helped raise our two sons, and ironed clothes to survive. Anything to make money.

In 2002 I started to learn about direct response marketing, and the new online industry of websites, Search Engine Optimization (SEO) and Pay Per Click (PPC) advertising with Google Ads (formerly AdWords).

Since 2005, I have been able to work from home (or my car, or hotel room, or at my children's school, or basically wherever I could get internet access by wi-fi or mobile dongle). My clients are world-wide businesses who pay me to run their Google Ads campaigns for them, since it's technical and complicated, and expensive (and all too easy) to get wrong.

Over time, the engineer in me found a way to build Google Ads campaigns that made my clients money and kept working reliably for months or even years with little intervention. My *micro-multinational* home-based business was born by accident.

And if people are using Google to search for your products and services, it's never been more important that you show up when people may want to give you money.

Wi-Fi Lifestyle

Among other travels, last year I did a three month, solo, around the world trip while working remotely. Clients continued to sell their stuff and make money while I was travelling. Clearly travel is impossible for the foreseeable future, but when I describe this wi-fi lifestyle and the ability to work from home for online clients, people's reaction is often "I want to be able to do that". And I'd love to teach you how!

There are certainly advantages and flexibility, you work what hours you choose, for clients you want to work with, there's no commuting, and you get more time with your family (although that can bring its own challenges!) Many of the tools, products and services you need to do it are either free or ridiculously cheap.

But there are also challenges and drawbacks, including and not limited to:

- Lack of regular pay with sometimes big ups and downs
- You're often hustling for new clients
- Clients leave reducing your income
- No paid sick leave, pension or holiday pay
- Your emotions can become a roller coaster

The biggest in my experience can be the solitary nature of the work, and it's essential you keep in regular contact with family, friends, colleagues and business groups. Fortunately, this has never been easier. If the pandemic had happened only fifteen years ago, our present situation would be unimaginably worse.

On balance, and although it was difficult adjusting from the corporate, office-based career I used to have (and particularly with two small children at the time) I much prefer the freedom and flexibility of remote and home-based working, with my own clients rather than an employer and a boss.

Your work and compensation can become more scalable rather than having to pitch for a pay rise which could never come. If you can continually prove your value to your clients, by making them money, then you should become permanently employable.

We have no idea what the new world after coronavirus will look like, and although businesses and people are having to adapt and adjust their work and lifestyle as never before, in the future humans will continue to trade, as they have always done.

The internet and working from home and remotely will play a bigger part in that than we ever suspected. And Google will continue to be the *digital match-maker* of choice for most people.

Listed below are the essentials I use to work remotely and from home:

A separate office space with desk

Originally, this was a desk in the main bedroom, but then I took over our smallest room where I could close the door and not be interrupted (sometimes embarrassingly like with small children or pets). A dedicated space feels more controlled, business-like and professional. Co-working spaces are great too. Find what works best for you.

Two large monitors

Once you try it, you'll wonder how you ever managed without, or just your laptop. I have two large Samsung monitors, one of which rotates to vertical which is great for working on slide decks or book-writing.

Laptop with 17-inch screen

I'm long-sighted so although it's heavier than a smaller screen I much prefer the larger size which is easier on my eyes, particularly when away from my two large monitors.

Additional (smaller) laptop

Really? Yes! If you're travelling and your laptop gets stolen, broken, lost or otherwise ruined, how will you be able to work? There may be internet cafes around, but I prefer the security and reassurance of an additional computer, and I have a Microsoft Surface just in case.

Additional mobile phone

Same reason as above.

Additional Wi-Fi network

As above. Sometimes your mobile can be your Wi-Fi hotspot.

Uninterruptible Power Supply (UPS) with battery backup

With power brownouts or failures, you risk device destruction and damaged software.

iPad Pro with attachable keyboard

Useful in confined spaces like aircraft where you can't open your laptop.

Dropbox (or Google Drive).

Business critical! Now all your files are available wherever you are. I work on my PC, then when I open my laptop, everything is synchronized and backed up. I can literally create a new computer from it with all my data and documents.

Video-conferencing - Skype or Zoom

I've been using Skype for free long distance calls for over a decade. Also useful for screen shares, call and video recording. Zoom is now becoming everyone's new best friend.

Microsoft Office 365 or Google equivalent

Goes without saying for document preparation and sharing.

Google Keep

Free note taking app which keeps all your notes synchronized across all your devices.

Google Chrome

My favorite web browser for many years, which can synchronize tabs across devices.

Gmail and Google Calendar

These were the game changers in 2009. Before I had been a Microsoft Outlook user, but going to the cloud for email and calendar was truly liberating.

Calendly

Free to get started, self-service appointment booking which integrates seamlessly with Google Calendar and Zoom.

Google Ads Editor

Specialized for campaign work.

Trello

The free version has enough functionality to collaborate with team members, and I haven't found anything better for storyboarding, outlining and sequencing.

Speed Dial 2 Pro

Bookmark manager which keeps all your bookmarks grouped and synchronized across your computers.

Bluetooth headset

For online conferences and phone calls.

High resolution webcam with mic

Your built-in laptop camera is not really good enough.

System Mechanic s/w

Keep your computers tuned up and performing.

AVG virus protection

Don't get infected.

Scrivener

Fantastic book publishing s/w.

A source of background music

Good company when working alone.

A large whiteboard

I'm visual and love to explore ideas by scribbling.

Xero online accounting and invoicing

I hate invoicing but this cloud solution makes it easy and has bank feeds, so all your transactions are easier to reconcile.

An accountant

A good help with bookkeeping and Xero.

Full online banking with cashback accounts and credit cards

I never use cash unless completely unavoidable, instead Barclaycard and Santander give me free money every month.

About David Rothwell

David Rothwell is a digital marketing and advertising expert with 15 years PPC experience with Google Ads (formerly AdWords), He grows online sales and revenue for world-wide B2B and B2C professional services, digital sales companies and eCommerce merchants.

His case studies span more than ten years and include business growth of 15x and Return on Investment of up to 20x. Qualifying clients can pay him a *share of the money created* on commission basis.

He is a faculty member and teaches for CEO Space International. He has spoken at conferences for Perry Marshall, Ken McCarthy, PPC Hero and TeCOMM.

He is the author of the *The Google Ads Bible for eCommerce* and co-author of the Amazon #1 best-seller *Sales Genius#1*. His upcoming online course *Clicks to Money - Making Google Ads Pay (No Agency Needed)* will be the new must-have for every business owner who hates paying Google.

https://www.linkedin.com/in/davidrothwellgoogleads/

http://davidrothwell.com/

Remote Working
RESET : RESTART : RESTORE your...

Padma Coram

The year 2020 has had a dramatic start thanks to Coronavirus. It has spared no one.

I believe working remotely is the new necessity and as a working individual, I truly believe every problem has a solution. This forced remote working may be the best thing to happen to us. The earlier we adapt to it, the faster we can get ahead of the curve.

I share below my experiences and strategies that helped me navigate through unexpected challenging times.

My Personal Background

I come from a deeply traditional scholastic Vedic Indian family. We can trace our lineage to well over two thousand years. All things *Mind, Body and Soul* is our way of living.

My Work Background

I started my professional career in three start-up companies in the Middle East - Emirates Airlines, MTV Middle East, and my own pioneering Entertainment and Events Company – a first for the Middle East. The entertainment business exploded shortly after into a multi-million-dollar industry, and the government came knocking to invest.

I later decided to step down to be a mother and work flexibly. I also moved countries from Dubai to London to be close to my son when he was a little boy in school. Moving to London was life altering. The extreme loneliness, the change in weather, lifestyle and culture paralysed me during the first few months. I had not prepared for this. I had to adapt quickly to retain my sanity. I was unsure how best to start a career in a new country with no support system and no friends. So, it was a no brainer for me to dip into what was natural and effortless to me, Lifestyle and Wellness - with Mindfulness, Meditation, Physical and Emotional Wellness being the core offering.

I started initially working from an amazing centre in Belgravia as a visiting consultant. My clients were ambitious, busy individuals but were unable to keep their appointments. I offered remote sessions as an alternative. With remote sessions, I had more clients signing up internationally. So much so, when the centre shut its doors permanently, the impact of the revenue loss from the centre and its clients was minimal.

What Is The Reality Of Working Remotely? What Are The Challenges? The Bad, Sad, And Ugly Bits?

Running our own business and working for ourselves is not just about working round the clock, we do that even as employees. It includes the added pressure and responsibility of knowing the buck truly stops with us. We simply have no one to ask for a bail out. We are constantly on surveillance mode and many lives depend on our every decision. There are no 'mental days off', we work remotely and in our head 24/7. We better be in love with what we do, or we could be heading for a nervous breakdown.

Being a one-man band and working out of a makeshift office initially was daunting. Add to the fact we have to generate revenue, create content, and make a dent in the market within the first few months to keep us afloat. Working from home meant no boundaries between personal or professional life. Personally, I did not know how to use the printer or fix any equipment. There was no dress code, structure or work schedule. I recall I had no opportunity to meet people for a coffee or catch up, and no colleagues to exchange ideas. I was unable to share my true fears with family.

I remember feeling lost. I recall crying and thinking what a big mistake I had made. I felt isolated and frustrated. It was a rude shock. I had a choice of giving up and heading back to familiarity. But I decided to stay and give it my all.

What Are The Advantages? The Benefits, Joy And The Good Bits?

After the initial mental adjustment, working from home introduces the liberty to be in relaxed clothes for a start. A relaxed person is a better person and is more efficient and effective. Saving travel time means we have more time to go for a walk, meditate longer, wake up later, or even have a full English breakfast. Saving hours and money, in commuting to work and back, especially in bad weather or rush hour is reason enough for many to work from home. Flexible working hours and working at our own pace beats fixed working hours hands down for me. Being with loved ones, as a mini break from the work desk, is re-energising. Working alone teaches us to multi-task, work smarter and faster. Personally, it became a joy to introduce my self-care routine as part of my work schedule, to be able to have healthy food breaks, quick yoga stretches and push ups between phone calls. I became a convert. To me the pros outweighed the cons very quickly.

How Do We Transition And Adjust To Remote Or Home-Based Working?

How do we get out of this merry go round of thoughts, anxiety, and freezing up? What initial advice and strategies do I suggest to my clients?

The answer is - Meditation and Mindfulness. This helps us be in a calm mental space and look at things from a place of clarity. Solutions flow from clear thoughts. I always say, the invisible is more powerful than the visible. To name a few - our emotions, our mind, and electricity are all not visible. For now, let's take coronavirus - invisible, dangerous and powerful.

Remember

- Mindset is everything and 90% of successful entrepreneurs always see the glass as half full no matter what.
- Focus on gratitude and start seeing situations with fresh creative eyes
- Everything we do comes from one space - our thoughts -
- When we think it's possible we create space for opportunities
- When we only see stuck points or fear we only see blockages to move forward
- When we feel stuck and like a victim of a situation, we hand over the control of our future

Self Questioning

Journal: Ask yourself these questions in stillness and silence every day for five days. Jot down the answers you get from within you.

- Am I being very rigid in my mental thinking?
  How can I loosen up?
- Am I creating more stress by the way I think? What if I let go?

- Am I 100% sure there is no way out? What would I do different if there was no fear of failure?
- Is this fear and confusion clouding my thought process? How would xx who I admire, handle this?
- Is this True? Really?

Spend two minutes on each question - for ten minutes daily for five days. Be honest with yourself. This exercise is for your benefit

Gratitude

Journal: Write down five good things about working remotely every day for five days. Read them on the fifth day. You will soon see endless opportunities and options.

From all the ideas you journal, highlight and pick the top five and start working and helping yourself. I tell my clients always *Keep the best, chuck the rest.*

Observe what remote working has allowed or opened your eyes to and give gratitude. See below for a few examples:

Day 1 (one example)

- Celebrating the freedom to be around loved ones
- Give four more examples

Day 2 (one example)

- Being able to have a hot home cooked meal
- Give four more examples

Day 3 (one example)

- One hour longer in bed in the morning
- Give four more examples

Day 4 (one example)

- The lack of office politics is liberating
- Give four more examples

Day 5 (one example)

- Adjusting work hours literally last minute to entertain a call or friend
- Give four more examples

Advice

Still stuck and confused, seek professional help. Learn how to meditate. This will be one of the biggest gifts you can give yourself. Approach a qualified, trustworthy professional to help you move forward. It's the best money you will invest. It will save you years of struggle when you work with the right professional. Research first and find the very best you can afford. In this case cheap is not a bargain. There is a reason the best cost more. They deliver results. Time saved is money saved and money earned. Errors in business are expensive.

Finally

Believe in you and think flexibly. Embrace change.

Replace fear and rigidity with fluid thoughts. *Keep the best - chuck the rest.* Remember the invisible is more powerful than the visible. Remote working opens doors to freedom, and endless possibilities

What we visualise can be created into reality. Invest in powerful, positive, productive thoughts.

There is NO BETTER TIME THAN NOW TO STEP INTO YOUR POWER. THE UNIVERSE WORKS WITH YOU WHEN YOU DECIDE TO STEP UP.

About Padma Coram

Indian born, London based Padma Coram is a multi-award winning Entrepreneur. Padma specialises in physical and emotional wellness therapy. She helps people manage stress and increase productivity through Meditation, Mindfulness and more. Her life's purpose is to empower and transform individuals.

Padma has personally been mentored by three self-made Billionaires, and individuals with high emotional intelligence like Mother Teresa, His Holiness the Dalai Lama, amongst many others.

Her clients range from young ambitious success oriented individuals, busy professionals, CEO's, politicians, royalty, and celebrities. Padma works remotely with her international clients.

Her motto is 'YES YOU CAN' whatever the issue.

"Padma is a great combination of the East and West. She is authentic and proactive and makes working together friendly and effortless. I recommend Padma. She is a champion."

Dr. Deepak Chopra

www.padma.live

Email: office@padma.live

LinkedIn: Padma Shankar Coram

Motivation – The Main Driver To Accomplish Anything When Working From Home

Marc Karschies

The famous cartoon character Dilbert by Scott Adams once asked an ethical question about telecommuting: "Do I owe my employer eight productive hours, or do I only need to match the two productive hours I would have in the office?" The answer given by Dogbert was that when factoring in how he is saving the planet by not driving, he would only owe one hour. While this is somewhat comical, it addresses some of the main concerns of telecommuting, working from home, home office, remote work, or whichever other name we want to give this concept of performing work activities form our own home (or outside the official workplace), and the wider societal benefits and organizational challenges that could come with it.

In general, there are several scenarios where a *working from home/remotely* situation could arise. As examples we can think of:

- Being in fulltime employment where the employer allows or requires the employee to utilize other than the company's premises to perform the work, either as a general arrangement and setup, or temporarily due to e.g. office closures as experienced during the Covid19 outbreak

- Working for oneself, e.g. as a freelancer or self-employed business owner, using the home as the office location either full time or after hours in addition to a more regular job
- Personal interest activities like performing a volunteering function from home, e.g. as involved parent for the kid's school or boy scouts, organizational function for sports clubs etc.

All of the above scenarios have some factors in common, e.g. how the working space at home could be organized to be most conducive to getting work done, what office equipment would be required, how communications are structured etc.

But they also differ in one significant point, what motivates the person working from home and the reasons for achievement and accomplishments. This in turn defines the necessary control and monitoring mechanisms for outcomes and how the work activities are actually structured and scheduled.

Common Factors

Let's start with some of the common factors.

To have an effective and efficient workspace, some key infrastructure needs to be in place. Adequate computer equipment, telephone connectivity, uninterrupted fast internet (e.g. fast enough for maintaining a strong video conferencing), printing and scanning, ergonomic seating, uncluttered dedicated and quiet workspaces etc. are the typical aspects and bare minimum raised in this regard.

However, aspects that are relatively easy to implement in a company work location at scale are often challenging or overlooked in a work from home setting. Examples include regular computer file backup facilities (in a home environment e.g. through automated easy to use cloud storage solutions like DropBox, OneDrive, iCloud), proper licensing of software, up to date virus and data protection software, IT support and time consuming office cleaning are often forgotten when setting up a home office and only become apparent when a disruption or inefficiencies occurs.

It is vital to ensure that minimum security requirements from employers or clients are implemented. Recent regulatory requirements in regards to data and privacy protection, and the increased hacking and phishing activities are only some of the aspects to keep in mind and adhere to. If it is deemed cost prohibitive or not possible to adhere to them for a small home office environment, then a work from home scenario is quite frankly not the right way to go.

Another frequent concern when setting up a home office, especially for self-employed work, is inadequate planning of volume and cost/benefit planning, which could lead to insufficient capacities or costly overcapacity.

A typical example are office printers where it is tempting to purchase the latest large office model with all imaginable features, but do you really need a A3 high capacity all in one colour laser printer, or is the existing low capacity ink printer potentially causing a bottleneck if several copies of high quality client presentations need to be produced at odd hours. It is often sufficient to cover 90-95% of the arising situations with own equipment, and for the remaining exceptions utilize one of the many providers of specialized support services (e.g. accounting, IT support, high volume or high quality specialized printing) available in the community.

Over the past years, communications and remote collaboration technologies have also significantly progressed. Systems like Zoom, Cisco Webex, Microsoft Teams, Chrome Remote Desktop, AnyDesk to name but a few, have made it easier for people to connect, collaborate and communicate virtually (voice and video conferencing included), share and collaborate on files in real time, establish virtual work spaces and activity tracking. However, the sheer multitude of systems on offer and speed of new developments makes choosing and keeping up to date with the available systems often challenging. While the system is usually prescribed and provided in an employment work from home scenario, self-employed working with a multitude of clients often face the situation that different clients require a variety of such systems, which could make licensing cost and keeping up the security more challenging.

Any type of inadequate infrastructure or downtime impacting productivity, or a perceived value impact will influence the motivation levels of the person working from home.

Motivation

As indicated above, motivation and the drive to accomplish when working from home is one of the most cited concerns when deciding to allow or start working from home.

In case of working on a volunteering assignment, motivation is usually extremely high as the volunteering work is often emotionally connected to the person. However, this could also lead to putting more effort in than actually required to achieve the necessary outcome. I have seen people design fully fledged relational database systems to store and maintain a list of less than 50 members of an interest group, something that could have been achieved with a simple list in Excel or Word at a fraction of the effort. Yet, because it is fun and aligned with one's personal interest, possibly coupled with peer pressure to show off high engagement levels, objectively more than necessary time and resources are spent on such assignments. But this is not the point in such scenarios. Volunteering is driven by the subjective personal positive feeling in spending time and effort for a cause one deeply cares about.

The above should make already clear that the personal motivations and engagement levels of people working from home are as diverse as they come. The opposite motivation scenario is often an employment relationship, where employers generally pay for time spent on company tasks, rather than personal interests. The motivation for the employee is therefore that of necessity and often more negative emotions, although there are arguably also many people that genuinely love their work and as such are easier to motivate than those who do not.

During the time *bought* from the employee, a certain set of accomplishments is required to be achieved. And here is the main difference of this scenario.

The organization needs to assign tasks to be completed that create the maximum value to the organization, at the lowest possible cost. Cost here are administrative, overhead, control and *non value-add but important* (to use a Lean term) activities, as well as unused time where the company failed to provide enough tasks to fill the worktime. In a work from home scenario, companies can save a wide range of administrative costs, e.g. workplace, telecoms, risks in regards to commute, less *socializing*, break times etc., as the employee is supposed to be measured on task accomplishments.

Employees on the other hand can often prioritize and schedule tasks in a way they feel most appropriate (triggering positive feelings and motivators). Positive for the employee is also that no unpaid time is spent on commute and that they have a certain flexibility on when break, start and finish times are taken, as long as the tasks assigned are completed. On the other hand, there is a strong risk of being side-tracked by things that are more motivating than the work, e.g. entertainment, family or pets, or the fridge, all potentially triggering a more positive feeling than uninspiring work.

Many companies fail to adequately estimate the correct time required to finish the assigned work, causing either unused time by the employee (see the Dilbert example above) or creating undue stress and unpaid overtime on the employees if they cannot complete the tasks within the allocated time. This can be e.g. due to slower connectivity, different processing requirements, more control and administrative tasks required when working from home etc.

Diverting too much from the full utilization on either side will cause dissatisfaction by either the employer or employee, often causing more control and management steps by the company to be implemented to monitor and (micro-)manage the work performed, further impacting the motivation levels of employees.

Due to the above, companies that have a highly engaged and empowered workforce, fair workloads, reasonable monitoring and controlling levels, higher levels of flexibility in scheduling and very clearly defined expectations on accomplishments to be achieved, are generally more successful in implementing work from home schemes. Those companies that do not adequately define workload and tasks, and leave too little flexibility and empowerment, often fail in their work from home initiatives.

This leaves the third group of people working from home, self-employed or freelancers. Here the motivation levels are often higher than with people in an employment relationship. This is due to the workers setting their own targets, knowing intrinsically what they expect themselves to be accomplished (less misunderstanding than in communicating between organization and employee), the benefits and risks are usually directly visible in financial and other business terms, and the work chosen is usually more aligned with the skills and interests of the person (why would the person otherwise start a business on this topic anyway).

However, impacts on the motivation are often through limitations on schedules and adequate planning, where either too many clients and too much work is taken on so that work life balance is impacted, or too little work poses an economic threat. The constant ups and downs of utilization levels and balancing between business development and actual work delivery often makes long term or consistent scheduling and routines challenging.

Here also short-term unexpected impacts due to non-working or failing infrastructure (as outlined above), can significantly increase stress and impact motivation.

Lastly, the potential lack of direct social interaction can cause psychological and motivation impacts, thus driving many work from home workers to schedule meetings or partially work from cafes or hotels or client sites.

Conclusion

When working from home it is important to find the balance between what is necessary and often demotivating on one side, and recognizing and celebrating or rewarding accomplishments, which can significantly improve motivation levels. Realizing where the motivation is coming from and what impacts or frustrates the motivation levels, and recognizing if that motivation is linked to an accomplishment can help finding that balance. Getting another snack from the fridge is not an accomplishment, but could be linked to an accomplishment if given as a reward after completion of a task, not only used as merely a procrastination attempt. Understanding which company policies, management actions and infrastructure failures are impacting motivation, and addressing them with the employer (or oneself), might help in increasing motivation and levels of accomplishments.

Overall it is therefore absolute vital to understand the targets to be accomplished, the impacting factors on productivity and what stands in the way of accomplishments, and what keeps one motivated, if a truly fulfilling working from home and work life balance is to be achieved.

About Marc Karschies

Marc Karschies, Managing Partner at KCA Consultants, is considered one of the leading experts on Corporate & Customer Experience Strategy and Integrated Service Quality Management in the MENA region. On top of his international consultancy work, he is a frequent expert speaker and award judge on CX and Service Quality Management & Strategy.

Before starting KCA's boutique CX consultancy and training business in 2013, Marc built a strong practitioner background with over 20 years in Financial Services incl. positions as Operations Director/VP at Diners Club Europe and Citibank International, and Head of Group Service Quality at Emirates NBD Banking Group. He is very active in the Dubai Quality Award and Dubai Human Development Award programs, and held various master level teaching assignments at HULT International Business School and Middlesex University.

Originally from Germany, Marc holds an Executive MBA from London Business School, a BBA in Finance and Banking (HfB Frankfurt), and a wide range of professional certifications, incl. Certified Customer Experience Professional (CCXP), ASQ Certified Quality Manager, Six Sigma Black Belt, and Kaplan-Norton Balanced Scorecard Certified Graduate.

Marc is co-author of the Amazon Best Selling book *Customer Experience*, sharing his current thinking on strategies and insights for achieving impact and visibility using world-class, best-practice CX principles (ISBN-13: 978 1912774418).

Website: www.kca-consultants.com

Twitter: KCA_Consultants

LinkedIn: https://ae.linkedin.com/in/MarcKarschies

Remote Working And Parenting

Dympna Kennedy

Working from home has always come with challenges, on the surface it's portrayed as a luxury, offering flexibility and better work life balance. The reality is very different, flexibility really means working into the night, while pretending it's all fine and easy. Recent events have seen many business owners and professionals thrust into working from home. For those already working from home it's gone from hardwork to the next level.

Working from home is nothing new in 2020.

Many professionals had the option before the arrival of Covid-19. Working from home can be a godsend when it comes to school drop-offs and pick-ups, and when a child is sick or absent from school.

In this new norm of social distancing, city lockdowns, and global disruption, what was once a necessity has become a non-negotiable. Scientific necessity dictates we bunker down, and that's caught many individuals and organisations unprepared. Classrooms and daycare centres are without their teachers and staff, gone is the luxury of compartmentalisation and schedules, and there's a new level of chaos about the home office.

Working from home amid a landscape that is rapidly shifting will present problems. It's very likely at times to be overwhelming, exhausting, and testing. You may experience doubt, fear, and a sense that you've lost some control. These are all perfectly normal reactions, and in this article, we're going to look at how you can prevent them from holding you back, stop them impacting on your relationship with stakeholders and colleagues, and learn to deal with shifting uncertain conditions.

In my work with parents, I often find that the most significant struggles stem from an inability to engage and communicate effectively with children. Many parents I talk to negotiate critical deals in their work daily. Some sign off on acquisitions, others work on major projects and manage multiple-teams. Yet they find negotiating with and managing a team of two under-fives almost impossible.

The success and recognition you have acquired professionally can mean nothing when faced with a stubborn two-year-old who flatly refuses to negotiate. Professionalism and manners go out the window in the case of a verbal five-year-old who doesn't feel like holding back when sharing what he thinks of you.

The insights that I want to share with you will help you maintain a semblance of sanity, and at the same time, you'll be building connections with your child. Busy working parents don't have the time to take on more. Most want a simple framework. A reference to help reflect, reset and recalibrate. That's where the SANE Framework® comes in. It's the quick reference guide for busy parents who are trying to remain sane in testing conditions.

The SANE Framework® Explained

S: Situation - the situation in which you now find yourself. You're either the parent who has previously worked from home or the parent assigned to working from home for the first time.

Whether you've been working at home previously or it's an entirely new experience, the difference now is that the bar has been raised significantly – and it's a whole new ballgame. It won't matter if you have the best internet connection around. The very latest ergonomically designed home office will count for nothing. Even a fantastic virtual support team won't save you if you've neglected to consider the most critical stakeholders of all – because kids have an uncanny ability to make your best-laid plans go pear-shaped.

If you're going to take one thing away from this chapter, just remember that it's easier to change the environment than to change the child.

You might like to consider:

- Think toys, too many and you risk overwhelming a child. That's often interpreted as boredom by adults.
- A useful guide for toys or books is to offer a familiar, a favourite, and one not seen for a while.
- Are they able to access water and healthy snacks?
- Do the children have their own clutter free space to study?

A: Acknowledge - your ability to acknowledge and bring on board all stakeholders will be critical to your success in working from home. That means checking on how you think, what you believe, and how you respond. What you say and what your child hears and believes can be very different. Can you identify the difference between "Wow! that is so good," "I'm so proud of you!" and "It looks like you gave that a lot of thought, you must be proud of yourself?" Acknowledgement doesn't mean you need to spend long periods with your child - it's about the smaller things. Showing an interest in what interests them, a thumbs up, a nod, a facial expression that shows delight -these are all moments of connection. The more you invest in connections, the higher the return will be, in the form of co-operation.

You might like to consider:

- Letting children know when you are working. They may believe you are just playing online
- Having regular times when you check in with them and showing your genuine delight to be back in their company
- Managing video calls and possible interruptions

Insight:

Children display a range of emotions throughout the day, and the younger they are, the more often mood changes can occur. Showing you're comfortable with their feelings, whether happy, sad, excited or frustrated teaches your child that they can turn to you for support and help. A young child needs to know that it's safe to show their emotions.

N: Neutral - this has proven to be the most challenging part of the framework because it calls on you to show your leadership qualities.

You will have moments where your buttons will get pushed, and you'll be tested; however, your ability to remain calm and composed will offer rewards.

The Circle of Security (COS) intervention refers to an inability to hold this balance as Limited Hands, losing the wisdom to stay in balance (Powell et al.). Children respond better to adults who acknowledge their feelings first, and then when they're calm enough, follow-up with logic. There will be times when your child wants to be in the office with you and will be disappointed, upset or angry when it's not possible. You may get tempted to respond with a bribe, threat or offer a reward – because they're all quick fixes. However, such methods are not ongoing or longterm solutions.

Acknowledge they're upset, *"I can see you are not happy"* lowers the intensity. *"You would rather be here with me?"*

reduces that intensity further. *"I would like that too"* (connection). Only at this point can you engage logic. Suggest an activity and say what you will do immediately after your call finishes, and then follow through with the promise. Acknowledge by focusing on an action taken by the child, *"Waiting here for me to finish must have been difficult, but you did it"* is more powerful than *"Good boy".*

You might like to consider:

- Reframing to realign
- Is she seeking attention, or is she in need of connection?
- Is his needing you a problem or an inconvenience?
- "Why are you doing this to me?" reframed as, "What do you need from me?"

Insight:

When you're trying to get through your work, you may just want your child to be good. A content child is a better goal than a good child. A child might be good out of fear, whereas a content child feels safe, valued and loved.

E: Envisage – we're all accustomed to living in an instant world. We have access to an unprecedented amount of information at our fingertips; we have an app for almost every situation. As a result, we're becoming more conditioned to expect instant results and quick fixes. Many parenting practices and beliefs deliver immediate results by employing threats and bribery. What I'm asking you to consider is the message that each of these ultimately sends to your children. Do we want them to believe that to get what you want in life, you should threaten or bribe others? In every interaction with your child, I want you to give some thought to the long term outcomes as opposed to short term rewards - this is your opportunity to influence future behaviours.

You might like to consider:

- You cannot give what you do not have. How are you taking care of you?
- Mistakes will happen, upsets will occur, but that shows your children you're human
- Project forward when stuck now and ask yourself, "Will this matter five years from now?"

Insight:

There has never been a better time to rewrite the parenting script to which you've adhered. Working at home is your opportunity to prevent any limiting beliefs from your childhood getting passed on to future generations.

Parting Thoughts

Within this uncertainty, I believe there is a unique gift for each of us, the opportunity to start again within our homes and create the change our world desperately needs; to pause, heal, connect and thrive.

What type of legacy do you want to leave your children? What memory do you want your child to hold dearest about you? What message do you want etched in their hearts that they will pass on to their children to share with future generations?

The actions you take today will have an impact on both your roles as a professional and a parent.

• Powell B and others, The Circle of Security Intervention: Enhancing Attachment in Early Parent-Child Relationships (The Guilford Press 2016)

About Dympna Kennedy

Dympna Kennedy is the founder of Creating Balance, a parenting and early childhood organisation dedicated to supporting parents and early childhood educators who are passionate about raising and educating young children. Dympna shares the innate power of non-verbal communication to help diagnose the real-time experiences of a child so that parents and educators can better understand each child's perceptions and needs. These insights result in a more connected, content and calmer child because they feel heard, valued, and that they matter.

Dympna is a recipient of the Family and Children's Services' Award for Excellence' for her research and work with babies and young children.

https://www.linkedin.com/in/dympnakennedy/

www.facebook.com/creatingbalanceglobal

www.creatingbalance.com.au

The Enlightened Entrepreneurs Guide To Working From Home

Kalpesh Patel

Did you know that reading speeds up your learning curve? Leaning on the experiences of others is the most efficient way to get from A to B, yet most try figuring it all out by themselves. Congratulations, for being the type of person that wants to learn and does that little bit more than most, I have learnt that these are the people that add the most value to society and get the most from this thing called, life.

I have read hundreds of books, co-authored in a few and written articles from time to time, no big deal unless you are me. As a creative dyslexic, I read very slowly and think very quickly. You can imagine how writing creates lots of frustration for me. Books have made such a huge difference in my life, I force myself to write in the spirit and hope of inspiring others. It's a love hate thing that pays off long term when I bump into people who have been infected and affected by my words in some way.

In this book, each chapter brings you a different person's perspective on remote working. I invite you to read each chapter with their lens on top of yours, step into their world to get the most out of it.

With that in mind, here are a few nuggets I hope will add to your daily inspiration as you step further into your personal journey, enlightening the entrepreneur within

1. Many Daydream: Entrepreneurs Work On Their Dreams.

The lens is that of a 14 months old child growing up in an entrepreneurial immigrant family that arrived in London in the 1970s. Picture me in this vibrant, high energy, colourful and loving surrounding of 30 family members sharing a 4-bed house in East London, they took the lowest paid jobs so they could pay the bills but the dream to be business owners once again was fuelled by a burning desire.

They were on a mission to be their own masters and as a result, there was always a side gig they were involved in, working 40 hours a week for a wage and another 40 hours a week for their dreams, this was the blueprint passed on to me. Whatever they may have lacked, they made up for in heart and disciplined life ethic.

I was born into a remote working family, it's in our culture and my DNA.

My forefathers left India over a century ago with a burning desire for a better life, it does not get more remote that this. Both my parents were born and raised in entrepreneur families in East Africa, they fled during Idi Amin's rampage of killing Indians in neighbouring Uganda. They packed their bags and took what they could, leaving their businesses and possessions behind. They arrived in England in the winter of discontent with no money, little language, no formal education and signs in the shop windows that read *No Dogs,No Irish and No Blacks allowed*. Put yourself in those shoes for a few seconds and see what miracles they produced with these ingredients.

If ever I'm feeling hard done by or sorry for myself, I think of them in these circumstances and the light of gratitude, hope and possibility are quickly re lit, feel free to develop the same mind mechanism for yourself, it really works.

"Dreams without Desire ... remain Dreams"

Kalpesh Patel

2. Just Do It.

I come from a heritage of four generations, raised on three continents, living with different races, languages, religions, deals, cultures, beliefs and thought processes.

It's impossible for me to quantify the value and advantages that their stories have given me, but I can tell you this, it is a blessing and gratitude that I recall daily.

I tell their stories to audiences all over the world now, to inspire greatness in humanity.

I started my first hustle at age 11 and never stopped. I have launched, built, bought, sold, flipped, invested, promoted, been lied to, ripped off, failed miserably, failed again and succeeded beyond any expectations in multiple businesses and helped thousands along the way.

If someone said it would not work, I'd look for a way, when it seemed too big for me, I'd look up for help, If it was something I didn't fully grasp, I'd find someone that did, I'd sacrifice personal gain to help others.

Consistency in Values is a great strength to develop, one that will give you an edge, long term. Develop your mind, language, personality and character, this was my edge over countless others that talk a great talk for a while and disappear as quickly as they came.

Be patient, there is no rush, you have your whole life ahead of you to develop yourself, it's a lifelong love affair. I have been blessed to have never had to work for someone else and thankfully only ever had to take half a dozen dole cheques in my 20s after bankruptcy, standing in that queue fired me up to start a telecom business with £200, it grew to over £35 million a year in revenue over 3 years. I had grand dreams of listing the company on the stock exchange that went very wrong, a story for another time.

I've made and given away or lost vast fortunes relative to most, built businesses with nothing in my pockets and scaled businesses to dizzying heights, now I love sharing the unique insights from such a fun and fearless journey.

What I value most is the relationships, freedoms and experiences life offers, these are always being added to my memory bank which is all we have left at the end of the journey.

"Build Faith in You"

Kalpesh Patel

3. The Future Belongs To Remote Workers.

We have already seen an increase in 4 day work weeks, home based business opportunities are experiencing explosive growth, the knowledge industry is surging, consulting, coaching, mentoring has flourished and if you are anything like me, working remotely is often abroad, my lap top and phone In tow and any beautiful balcony or sea front cafe on a sexy beach is the office for the day.

We are living in an era that needs more flexibility, talent, skills, ability and insights.

We are experiencing a global metamorphosis.

The introduction of quantum speed computers and Artificial Intelligence will bring the internet of things alive in ways we have not dreamt up yet, all of this is pointing towards a completely new world within decades, it will make the last three decades look like 3 centuries. We are the first group of humans that are experiencing breakthroughs at unseen speeds.

The idea of surviving independently is a tough one for most to grasp, the sooner we embrace it the better for all. When you work remotely, there are many self-destruct mechanisms to look out for. They often make a huge noise when you try something different but sometimes, they hum so quietly we cannot identify them. This can lead to all sorts of doubts and mental sickness, learning to manage this chatter is a huge advantage if you are to survive the long game of remote working.

Here are a few critical daily practices, they require conscious effort to start with, if consistent, over time they will become your natural habits.

- Set reminder alarms for Regular Breaks for Me Time
- Deep Breathing Exercises, Stretching, Mindful Awareness, Hydrating, Nourishing the Body and the Mind.
- Set Reminders to get the work done too, it's easy to do nothing and the day fly by, which is fine if that was the plan is for that day.

I highly recommend the Audible App for access to ongoing and updated materials, it's currently my best friend.

Knowing that the future is changing faster than ever, why not prepare in advance?

Start today, start now.

"Foresight is better than Hindsight"

Kalpesh Patel

4. Find Your People

I'm proud to acknowledge that everyone that shared that 4-bed house, educated their children, own their own homes and businesses and many have retired happy while the children continue to build on their shoulders. If they ALL did it, it was not down to luck alone, they lovingly supported each other in every sense of the word, united as one, they shared similar ideals and dreams, they had similar work ethics and followed a proven system that worked.

Thankfully, these days there are more than enough free or low-cost online groups, local meet ups, networking opportunities, mastermind groups, business clubs and communities, entrepreneur opportunities and so on that you can plug into.

Getting your mind set tuned in is an art, thankfully, there are hundreds of great books about this too. Remind yourself that working remotely does not mean working alone.

Make the effort to meet those further ahead on your path and bring those behind you along too. Do not forget the importance of social interactions too.

All work and no play makes Kalpesh a very dull boy.

Find out who is where you want to be and step into their light. Learning these skills is not difficult once you commit, take the first step and the next step is more likely to follow.

"Choose your Tribe Wisely"

Kalpesh Patel

5. An Untrained Mind Steals Possibility

At age 16, I was making more profit in my lunch hour than many adults made for a full days work. I could not understand why they carried on doing something that was giving them less than they were capable of. I'd wonder if I was better than them, more than them, was I the chosen one?

At some point I realised it was none of that, they simply had not learned to see the world the way I had. I had developed a different way of thinking, seeing, hearing, experiencing and processing life than they had. We just had different lenses, my world view and theirs was the same but appeared different.

When I shared my Utopian thoughts, ideas and dreams and spoke of the future we could create if we joined forces and made changes, they laughed or ignored me as if I'd lost my mind. I soon learnt only to share it with those that showed similar traits.

The older I got I noticed just how inefficient most people and businesses were. I would think of the life my parents talked to us about and realised that this was a gift I had inherited. Most people lacked vision, belief, confidence and most importantly... the desire to progress. Today I share how shifting your perspective changes everything, change your lens and see what you've been missing that was always there.

This works in relationships, careers, businesses and most importantly, how we perceive and relate to ourselves.

"Self-Awareness is the best gift you can give to the world"
Kalpesh Patel

6. Entrepreneurs Never Give Up And Always Get Back Up

In my early 20's I used to buy and sell cars, I purchased empty or run down shops and flipped them for profit, I thought I was invincible. Then adversity struck, I lost my superhero, my father when I he was just 51, it wiped me out of the games of life. I was financially, emotionally and spiritually smashed. I lost my faith in a higher power and lost hope in myself.

I went on to become an angry, resentful and bitter human being. I distanced myself from family and friends, self-punishment was my new way of life. I lived in dark thoughts and was always out getting drunk. I soon broke up with my high school sweetheart of 6 years and my business went bankrupt within 15 months.

This went on for 3 years until I was introduced to Personal Development in a Network Marketing company. I met my tribe, made new friends, was inspired and mentored by great leaders and started living again.

These last two decades I have turned my experiences and lessons into a speaking and training business.

It allows me to travel as an inspirational storyteller, I've been blessed to have advised several direct sales companies, trained over 700,000 people at live events, helped thousands to work from home full time.

I share this in the hope to inspire something in you, trigger a spark that's waiting to be lit up so that you can excel in whatever path you pursue. If it happened to me, it can happen to you.

I never take my journey for granted and share as openly as I can to help as many as I can.

I remind myself daily just how blessed I am to own my time and my mind, empowering and inspiring humanity inspires me.

I hope this has accelerate your learning and helps you to make the transition in a smoother and more succinct manner. The entrepreneurs in this book have been through a road less travelled, one that you are about to embark on, and we share openly because we all know… It's not easy, but it is most certainly worth it.

Look forward to the future adventures.

With Love and Gratitude.

About Kalpesh Patel

Kalpesh Patel is listed on the top 50 inspirational speakers alongside Tony Robbins, Brian Tracey and Les Brown. He specialises in Leadership, Sales and Peak Performance Life Strategies. His success is built around his passion for making a difference and transforming lives, training people on optimising their mind for peak performance.

He is also a documented million dollar a year-earner in the Direct Sales Industry with over $500m in personal team sales volume and teams of over 100,000 people globally in two decades.

Kalpesh has built his own companies in retail, telecommunications and events. He has developed dynamic training systems and leadership training courses to help Sales companies and teams to expand globally.

He has mentored dozens of start-ups on effective leadership and communication and trained high-level staff to maximise output from teams and improve company profits.

Kalpesh also Co-founded *www.WTOHub.org* and *www.WeInspireYou.com* with two friends and they have a dream to build the world's biggest *Difference Making Personal Development Community.*

Connect with Kalpesh Patel on:

LinkedIn https://www.linkedin.com/in/thekalpeshpatel/

or call him on +447956436703

Cake Making To Handcrafted Leather Shoes

Marcia Brown

Why I Started Working From Home

Working from home started approximately ten years ago. I was offered redundancy on a number of occasions because the workplace was relocating. Eventually, I welcomed the opportunity not knowing what my employment position would entail in the forthcoming weeks ahead.

As time went along and after searching the internet for ideas, my interest was heading in the direction of cake making! I started to visit one particular cake shop each day for many weeks. The visit to the cake shop became a daily trip, in fact it became an obsession a thrill and a need which gave me much joy.

My daily viewings of cakes in the shop window encouraged me to bake a cake which I presented to my friend for her birthday, she was overjoyed and loved the presentation of the cake.

The cake making venture was shared with other friends and within several months I was making several cakes per week which was purchased by friends and colleagues to begin with.

Being new to the cake industry was challenging because I was still in the very early learning stages, however this catapulted into regular cake orders and development of a skillset embedded deep inside my very soul that was not yet apparent.

My specialist area of cake making development became a presentation of techniques displaying moulding, carving, choosing great colours and producing cakes of high quality and great design.

My clientele changed as my expertise grew producing unique decorative cakes to the highest standard.

My cake specialist area was handbags and shoes cakes, the shoes started as mini handcrafted ornaments. As time went along together with clients requesting larger shoe ornaments my skills developed into lifelike ornamental shoes for cake tops.

Within three years of cake making from home, together with administration, certificates and qualifications I felt the time was right to further develop the business. The Ornament shoe making cakes started to become more developed with embellishments and design.

My next project was the development of Designerart Cakes Shoe kit which consisted of a video, patterns, step by step guide, cutters, heel mould with skewers and a shoe kit box to complete the presentation.

With the majority the items already in place, it was just a case of making large quantities and updating into a workable project. With assistance, advice and research it was decided that two of the items would be manufactured internationally.

This project involved investment, so as a result had to find a buyer for the shoe kits, eventually I found a wholesaler who advertised the shoe kit in their catalogue therefore giving a timeline of three months for delivery to their warehouse ready and waiting for clients to purchase.

This was a challenge to meet all criteria, correct processes and produce all relevant documentations. Requests locally and internationally meant being awake night and day to remotely ensure the specifications of all items were as required. This was done by receiving pictures every step of the way until the prototypes were ready and agreed.

The timeline for delivery of the project was fast approaching the deadline however After further discussions I was informed a contingency plan was already in place, which allowed their clients to place back orders for the shoe kits. The shoe kits were packaged and delivered from my home address with great success and feedback.

Events that occurred after the launch of the kit included attending the NEC Birmingham as a stall holder at the Cake International Event selling Designerart Cakes Shoe Kit, appearing in magazines, being a participant of a TV programme People Who Stop at Nothing to Be the Best.

In closing this chapter of the shoe kit development never give up, when it seems all Is lost pick up the phone and talk, if you have a brilliant product your skillset will move mountains.

At present the shoe kit has slowed down however the entire experience has been great in terms of my development in administration, product design and production. It gave me confidence to engage with people from all walks of life locally and internationally all from the comfort of my home has been amazing.

What Am I Doing Now?

Up to date I am no longer making cakes, the shoe kit business is in the process of being sold

We are now in March 2020, approximately 18 months ago a colleague visited my home and saw the various sugar crafted shoes on display.

I was then challenged to find a leather shoe course.

I attended a ten day course on making shoes where I gained basic shoe skills only.

This course set my creative juices on a path of excitement, passion, hunger for learning more, researching which would lead to effectively making leather shoes from home.

The progress started with visiting Lineapelle Italy and Futurmoda Spain Leather Accessories and Shoe Components Show. At both events It was great to engage with suppliers, shoemakers locally and internationally and to especially learn, learn, learn, I was like a child in a sweet shop, it was then I actually found my calling!

The next stage of progression was to learn about the various machinery that would ultimately lead to making leather hand- crafted shoes from home using minimal tools.

I was also fortunate to access the shoemaking online course program delivered by Sveta Kletina. It has so far given me the technical ability to pattern make, cut and sew shoe uppers, last and complete various shoe design to an exceptional standard.

To learn pattern making requires great patience and the technical ability in following the laws of construction in shoe making. To cut requires precision and almost perfection, to sew also requires perfection almost like learning to drive a car, and to last requires attention to detail.

I had to be savvy, so whilst learning to make various shoe designs, it was a case of multitasking on all other areas of development.

Within six months of progression, it was decided to locate a mentor to assist in the development of the brand. This project that lasted approximately four months and was a fast track situation due to lack of finances.

By now there was a number of outstanding projects and grey areas that needed to be completed. After some quick thinking and research was I able to attend a five day training course at the university of London to finally complete and access further knowledge. This was a fantastic Christmas present every day of attending the course was greatly exciting due to the course tutor being over and above exceptionally informative with his standard of teaching and techniques.

This now enabled the completion of a collection of shoes and a photography session.

During this time a website was in the progress of being made, the shoe pictures assisted in the go live of the website

wwww.marciabrownfootwear.com

What Is My Unique Selling Point?

I currently have bunions and was fed up as I could not find shoes to fit.

Through sheer determination can now sit at home and make myself a pair of shoes to accommodate my challenging feet.

Commissions since Christmas is as follows:

- A pair of flat ballet patent leather shoes for a lady who has size 8.5 very narrow feet.
- A lady who is size 6.5 with wide feet
- A lady who requires a size 2 wide feet trainers
- Along with potential collaborations locally and internationally.
- Whilst still learning to make trainers, ladies and men Oxford shoes

Conclusion

Working from home can be exceptionally rewarding, relaxing, development of what you do best, encouragement and inspiration to others.

All you need is determination, do not let money decide in your ability to process any uncomfortable situations, there is always an answer to the problem. When overwhelmed keep going by processing easy projects this will free up your mind to move on to any other challenges and obstacles.

When you are tired get lots of sleep this will assist your thoughts and ability to think clearly.

Keep your work at home hours Monday to Friday so you have downtime to relax and enjoy life. In my downtime I am a support worker at weekends, I have a great time and feel honoured to be able to contribute and help those in need.

It has been a great pleasure sharing the working at home experience it has been a wonderful and interesting journey every step of the way. At no point would I have ever imagined making shoes cakes would progress to making leather shoes from the comfort of my home. The process has been like a jigsaw puzzle where does the next piece fit.

About Marcia Brown

Marcia Brown is the CEO of Marcia Brown Footwear Ltd which provides handcrafted leather shoe designs to clientele seeking limited edition and people who have sizing challenges with their feet.

The shoes are comfortable, display clever placement of fine embellishment specially handmade in her London atelier

A solid relationship with Italian and Spanish manufactures allows the bespoke maker to select exquisite quality material and deliver bright great co-ordination in her designs.

With Creative talent and conscientious quality of service, the designs display a diversified product line inclusive of evening wear, elevated heels, flats as well as trainers for all shoe fashionistas.

wwww.marciabrownfootwear.com

Instagram: marciabrownfootwear

Instagram:shoecollectables

Turning Weakness To Strength

Luke Murfitt
UK Entrepreneur Of The Year

In January 2018, Luke had no job, no prospects and no profile.

Two years later – despite Parkinson's disease and working from home – he won the UK Entrepreneur of the Year at the UK Business Awards. But that isn't all.

Two years into his journey Luke:

- Launched a company in a sector he didn't know (against 33,000 competitors)
- Grew the business by 650%
- Won a six figure contract he had no chance of winning (on one of London's biggest new builds in Canary Wharf)
- Saved money by paying staff more
- Helped 39 mothers back into work (and 9 fathers)
- Became a Global Ambassador and International Keynote Speaker
- Excelled through COVID-19 by offering a daily business disinfectant service
- Launched 'Global Futurists' business Podcast
- Learned to draw strength from his disease

How was this possible in 24 months? With his Positive Mindset, Luke shares the story of his home based company – Integrity Cleaning & Integrity Virus Control – and the realisation that changed his life.

An office or place of work is usually seen as a worthy investment, an unavoidable, justifiable fixed cost that is not questioned. This separate address for many, forms an identity, it creates a sense of pride and for start ups is seen as a qualification to prove to clients and peers that you are credible. For a SME business owner, an office away from home creates a boundary to separate work from personal life. Locking the office door at 5:30 allows the owner to mentally switch off and come Friday, turn off until Monday morning.

This is all reasonable, acceptable and fine.

BUT what if you saw the 30 min journey time to, and from the office as stolen time? One hour a day is 261 hours a year, that's 29 days of work a year lost to driving to and from *the office.*

Now what if you wanted to work into the evenings and Saturdays? Rest is good, and should be a sought, but so is accelerated success, achievements and being better ... than the *rest.*

An extra three hours in the evening and six hours each Saturday creates an additional 1,005 hours a year. That with the driving time means an additional 150 (9hr) office days available to building your business. To an Entrepreneur that is music to my ears.

Meanwhile, saving £12,000-15,000 p/a running an office plus travel costs, at 30% net profit is £40,000 a year less in sales required. Investing such into a business development manager instead = more growth! Running a company with fewer fixed costs is also very helpful should a unforeseen challenge come along - like COVID-19.

Reduce your risk.

I fully recommend a garden log cabin office, which I will be obtaining soon but now I want to take you on my journey over the past two years, and the 7 steps I take every morning that have helped shape my winning mentality, positive mindset and life.

Legend

In January 2018, I had no job, no prospects and no profile.

What I had was a family, a mortgage and a plan.

And one other thing – Parkinson's disease.

It had been three years since the diagnosis, and time was not on my side. I'd been a FTSE 100 Sales Manager. Now I was standing outside a Job Centre.

I remember that morning. It was dark and dismal, but I had hope. The queue stretched out the door. People without work. People claiming benefits.

I walked towards the entrance, my foot dragging slightly.

Parkinson's is like moving through treacle. It attacks your central nervous system. Getting to my feet is a challenge. Getting dressed is a challenge. But it can only take your strength.

Your state of mind is up to you.

And I had learned something powerful from the disease. Often, weakness can be turned into strength.

Inside the building, I told them my plan.

"I want to build a business. I want to hire the people outside."

They smiled and nodded, watching the tremors in my hand. I showed them my briefcase. The documents. The spreadsheets. The logo. It was my dream business - a commercial cleaning company.

They smiled some more and asked what a Sales Manager knew about cleaning.

I laid it all out.

Cleaning is a dirty business. An industry ripe for disruption.

33,000 competitors in the UK.

Low margin. Low wages. Poor staff. Poor service.

But this wouldn't just be any cleaning company.

This would be Integrity Cleaning.

More than a name. It was a mission statement.

I wanted to help people back into work.

I wanted to change lives by paying a living wage.

Better pay would mean better staff, better work and better service.

A virtuous circle. Weakness turned to strength.

When I finished talking, they smiled some more and showed me out.

It was okay. They didn't know me.

I began signing up mothers who wanted to work.

It wasn't just the money that attracted them.

We offered training, flexible hours and most of all – respect.

All we needed was the first client.

Four months later, we launch, it happened – a contract with a hotel. Then another and another and another.

Integrity was working, but I needed help.

I took on a business coach and an investor. They both got it.

We weren't just winning contracts; we were changing lives.

They both invested in us, and we invested in our people.

That's what Entrepreneurs do. They lead a team of winners.

We talked to them, listened to them and learned from them.

With no remote office, Integrity took off.

In November 2018, I walked onto a building site at Canary Wharf. Seven towers. One-thousand apartments. Each one worth a million pounds. The elite developers were famously hard to win over, but I didn't know that.

I just asked to see the person in charge.

Seven weeks later, we won the tender. A million square feet of cleaning.

That's when the media took an interest.

I was on the radio one day and in the papers the next.

Yes from day one, we had an official office address, a website, 0800 Tel no, Ltd, VAT, a Brand, Embroidered shirts, photos, systems, templates, methods and many wonderful cleaners.

Apart from Gods blessings our number one weapon was a sheer passion and positive mindset

It was easy. I just talked about our people, our culture and values. I talked about turning weakness to strength.

In June 2019, the Job Centre nominated me for the UK Business Awards.

More radio. More press. More opportunity to inspire.

No physical office, no problem!

The applications. The presentations. The questions from judges.

On the day of the awards, I stood up in front of the judges and laid it all out.

650% year on year growth. 3,500 apartments cleaned. Thirty-nine mothers back into work.

But the judges didn't just hear success; they heard my philosophy, my passion, and my story. And they gave me a standing ovation.

That night, at the ceremony, I waited with bated breath. Our table was between Virgin and Manchester United.

70 finalists. All eyes on the stage.

"And the winner of UK Entrepreneur of the Year... is ..."

"LUKE MURFITT!"

As the applause grew, I leapt onto my chair and punched the sky. But it wasn't just a win for me. Every person in my story owns that award. The mothers. The mentors. The investors. The clients.

I remember the excitement and love in the room – the warmth, all that hard work, dedication, long hours at home and belief - paid off!

That warmth has never gone away.

Integrity Cleaning goes from strength to strength, but there's more to do.

When you see how a simple story can change lives, you have a responsibility to act.

In January 2020, I became a Global Ambassador for Awards International. Now I Keynote speak at national and European events, podcast (Global Futurists) from home and spread my message of positivity around the world.

And do you know what makes me smile?

People think I've done this despite the Parkinson's...

But they couldn't be more wrong.

This is the life that gets me out of bed in the morning.

Getting up is a painful challenge, but inside I'm happy.

And when I reach the bedroom door – fifteen minutes later – I raise my arms above my head.

I feel blessed and thank God for the new day.

Because it doesn't matter how long it takes to get there.

By the time I walk through, I'm already a winner.

Ready to look beyond myself.

No office, no problem - positive mindset and a winning attitude will get you far.

Finally - my top 10 tips of working from home:

1. Dream BIG then wake up, get up and chase them!
2. Begin your day with Thanks and a Positive mindset
3. Get dressed
4. Use To-Do Lists, block out / plan diary and have routines
5. Avoid TV, games consoles and the biscuit tin
6. Leave the house every day - meet a client or coffee with spouse
7. Get a good business card and 0800 tel. no.
8. Aim for a Garden Log cabin
9. Get a good business coach and or mentor
10. Stay focused and THINK BIG !

About Luke Murfitt - UK Entrepreneur of the Year

In January 2018, Luke Murfitt had no job, no prospects and no profile. Two years later – despite Parkinson's disease and working from home – he'd won the UK Entrepreneur of the Year at the UK Business Awards. Luke is a leading entrepreneur and professional speaker

Website: www.IntegrityCleaning.co.uk

Keynote: www.LukeMurfitt.com

Linkedin: LukeMurfitt

Podcast: 'Global Futurists' www.cxm.co.uk/global-futurists/

The Stress–Free Working From Home AdVICE

Su Patel

Introduction

Have you ever felt like the rug had been pulled from underneath you?

Well, if you were with me in April 2016, you would find me sitting in my car sobbing, uncontrollably, not because I just handed over the keys to my house to the new owner, but because I felt like my world had been turned upside down, you see this was the house that I had the best years of my life with my husband and daughter, living every girl's dream of, having it all – the family, the home, the career and the lifestyle, which gave me the security I always wanted.

But, just 2 months ago, in February, I had walked out from my marriage of 10 years, it just wasn't working, but I knew that I would be OK as I had a secure job, only to find out in March, that I was faced with redundancy from my 27 year corporate job at Tesco.

So, you can imagine, I had reason to be a bit upset, I was petrified about my future, my daughter's future.

The emails stopped, the phone calls stopped, people that I knew from work disappeared, my immediate family lived an hour and a half away and I suddenly found myself with a lot of time spare with nothing to do and no one to speak to.

I had defined myself based on the job I did, the money I made, who I worked for, the fact that I was married and having a loving family and now that it was all gone, deep feelings of worthlessness took over.

"I have nothing, I'm worth nothing, I just feel like giving up!!

"Don't be silly Su, you're strong and you're going to get through this and think of Pia, you have to be strong for her!" My brother didn't like seeing me like this. I was the tough one, I was the strong one. But the truth was, I was tired of being strong. I was tired of being anxious about the future and tired of always having to be strong.

But the thought of giving up and not taking responsibility would mean that someone else would have to take responsibility for me, would it end up being my daughter?

I couldn't do that to her, I knew my mind was spiralling downwards and I realised that was the first thing I needed to work on.

As you know, there are many personal development tools and information out there to build a strong mindset, but information wasn't what I needed, I needed implementation.

I remembered the name Tony Robbins from a few years back and I found a few of his videos on YouTube, I started watching them as much as I could, every time I sat down to eat, I would watch his video and take an action. Whether it was to read another book, journaling or go to my yoga class or write in my gratitude diary. This was just the beginning of me taking ownership.

Coming from a corporate background of 27 years, I was used to being busy all day, a long list of things to do and now that I am home, the guilt was setting in, "Should I be doing more work?" Should I be working 9-5?" Will I be seen as unproductive and lazy?" "Will I achieve what I need to if I wasn't working every single hour of the day?" And I didn't feel worthy not being needed by others.

I realised that it was going to take something of me to master being at home and in charge of my own hours. "Am I really not required to be part of the rat race, the commute, the Monday morning blues and be around people that I didn't like?" A completely new paradigm, is it really going to be OK to go to a yoga class at 9.30am or the gym at 2pm? I started seeing the possibilities for me.

With this newly found freedom and being the owner of all of my time, I easily got distracted doing things that I liked to do rather than needed to do. It was easier to do the washing and hoovering rather than make a plan. It was easier to not go to the gym and take a lunchtime nap. It was easier to catch up with friends than look for opportunities.

I followed these four steps to create an amazing life working from home.

Step 1 - Vision

I realised that I was really blessed with time to learn and get my 'house in order' I came across the 'wheel of life' and looked at all areas of my life; my health, my finance, my development, my career, my relationships, my family, my environment and my contribution to others. Needless to say, everything was out of balance and I was dissatisfied in every area of my life.

I became lazy, stuck and unproductive and hated it. So, I knew that to do more and have more I needed to BE different. I created that who I needed to be was disciplined, focused and consistent if I wanted to achieve my vision. But what was my vision?

I was at ground zero so I knew that I could create anything I wanted, I created, not just a vision board seeing a business with clients, amazing health and a fit body, a vision of beautiful destinations for a holiday, spending time with family, meditating and having lots of money, but also, a vision of who I wanted to BE for others.

Step 2 - Integrity

After doing the Landmark Forum with Landmark Worldwide in 2017, I learnt a lot about integrity and being my word. There were so many things that I promised myself that I would do something and hadn't done it, I hadn't followed through and taken responsibility for.

What I learned was that as human beings we are nothing but our word. We create everything in language and once we have given our word to something, we have a responsibility to be our word, when we are not being our word we diminish the listening that others have of us and also diminish how we listen to ourselves.

This gave me the inspiration and empowerment to create a listening of myself to be the kind of leader that says and does what they say they will do. To be a credible, respected and confident leader. Discipline, focus and consistency was going to get me there.

Step 3 - Commitment

Knowing what I was committed to was going to take being - disciplined, focused and consistent. I knew I needed more routine in my life, so I created a schedule and as Tony Robbins calls it, I designed my 'hour of power'. I started waking up at 5.30am, working out, doing yoga and meditation, focusing on my goals daily and writing out my actions for the day in all areas of my life, not just for work, but also for connecting with my family, friends, connections, personal development, health and ensuring I was being my word in those areas.

There have been times where I have let self-doubt and negative emotions creep back in, overwhelm me and want to give up but I have an amazing team who I call my circle of influence around me, these are people that I aspire to be like, mentors, coaches, colleagues who want me to succeed, sometimes more than me. They will not let me give up and will not listen to me as anything less than a miracle for the world. That does mean that, I have to listen to some hard truths sometimes but hear it with their love present in every word. There is a saying that goes *If you are the most successful person in the room, you are in the wrong room.*

Step 4 - Educate

Technology has certainly simplified my life and embracing new ways of doing things is a trait that I learnt from my Tesco years of a fast-paced business.

I only started using Facebook properly about four years ago, being alone in Southend-on-Sea without my family and friends, I stay connected with people and engage with people that I have never met, this has breathed life into my sense of self-expression.

I am usually reluctant with new technology at first, it's the fear of the unknown, however I have challenged myself to embrace it and find people who have used it to train me. The more technology I familiarised myself with, the more freedom and time I created for myself. Step by step process always works for me and there is no rush. Create a habit of continuous learning, from others, books, podcasts, articles, online courses, attend webinars and seminars.

Conclusion

Success is how YOU define it. There is no other way to measure it. My success is that I have the health and body I want through my fitness routine, I have number of successes since working from home - I am a published author of *Putting The Human Back Into HR – Success as a HR professional begins with you,* I have spoken internationally in Barcelona, the Maldives and in Rome, I have become a key person of influence in the area of personal development and leadership for HR professionals, I have beautiful relationships with my family and friends, I enjoy life with my new partner and my daughter is happy and healthy.

Above all, I have complete freedom and peace of mind, but it takes being disciplined, focused and consistent.

About Su Patel

Su Patel is the founder of The HR Leadership Academy, Author of *Putting The Human Back Into HR – Success As A HR Professional Begins with you!* A Keynote Speaker at international HR events including Barcelona, The Maldives and Rome.

She started her career in 1988 with one of the biggest retailers in the UK, and after twenty-seven successful years she took a redundancy package. She now shares her experience with a wider audience, empowering HR professionals globally to provide a world-class, human-centred approach.

Su understands that working in HR can be quite challenging. Finding the right balance between what the business needs and doing the right thing for employees is no easy task for a HR professional. Her training programmes are designed to focus on the practical and people-focused reality of working in HR.

Su says 'when HR is confident, they can be credible and proud of their contribution - helping people and businesses grow"

Connect with Su Patel on:

Linkedin www.linkedin.com/in/coach-for-hr-professionals

Make Sure That Remote Working Supercharges Your Culture - And Doesn't Stall It

Phil Lewis, Corporate Punk

Culture is the social order of an organisation. It describes the narratives, processes, ways of thinking, values and behaviours that inform what gets done, when, and how.

Metaphorically speaking, culture might be regarded as the operating system of a company. It often remains hidden and unacknowledged – but it hums away in the background and has a direct bearing on the functioning of every single process in the machine. (In this context you can also substitute 'process' with 'people'.)

For as long as the concept of work has existed, culture has been forged as a result of an ongoing, often implicit negotiation between people sharing a physical environment about how they prefer to co-exist. Human beings are social creatures. We are neurologically programmed to want to be part of a tribe – and to want to work in ways that are acceptable to that tribe. Culture grows as a direct consequence of these desires. Every individual in an organisation influences culture in some way (although some are more influential than others, by dint of their position in the tribe).

Remote working – a long-standing promise of the revolution in work that technology is enabling – is now an urgent challenge for many organisations. And it can pose a threat to culture for one simple reason: while the shift to remote working is highly visible, the lack of meaningful attention paid to culture by most leaders makes its impact hard to quantify and manage.

So, how do you preserve and enhance your culture when your people are no longer physically together?

The answer lies in a simple framework called the 4 Cs, which identifies the main pillars of successful remote working: contextual clarity, companionship, conflict management and communication. This framework – which my practice, Corporate Punk, has developed and tested with leading organisations around the world – provides a foundation for leaders to continue to design and manage a culture in which their people can perform at their brilliant best, regardless of physical location.

Because here's the thing: remote working is not just like in-person working with added Zoom.

Contextual Clarity

Contextual clarity refers to how well a workforce understands what is happening and why. The golden rule: in the absence of such clarity, people are likely to believe the worst or the weirdest thing. Human beings are meaning-making machines; without a straightforward narrative, we are prone to all kinds of make-believe.

It's critical for leaders to ensure they communicate regularly and provide context. Time-poor leaders who are struggling to navigate change challenges often neglect this critical aspect of cultural management. Remote working is itself a change challenge, but here it also acts as a force multiplier: isolated individuals are more likely to start making up stories than they are when they're with others.

The result of low or no contextual clarity? A lack of unification in the culture, and a wholly inefficient operating system.

The first fix for remote working: ensure that you have a daily all-hands conference call, to update on major developments, address exceptional issues and set expectations. Convening a longer huddle each week is also advisable.

Companionship

Remote working can challenge our innate need for human warmth and connection – a need on which the world itself turns. Every day, in every office, you can witness countless acts of companionship – from people making drinks for colleagues to casual enquiries about the weekend; from handshakes to hugs.

Relegate companionship and you relegate a vital sense of connection to others. In an organisational context, this will dilute the humanity of a culture and, as a result, a sense of shared engagement in the company's mission and values. Smart leaders facing the need for remote working will seek to compensate for this. In simple terms, if you can't make a coffee for a colleague or hug them hello, what can you do instead?

For a start, you can quit believing that every interaction has to be exclusively business-focused. Instead, consider how you create an environment in which your people can interact without any implied performance pressure. (This might be a channel on Slack, or smaller team Zoom calls with no agenda.)

The first fix for remote working: Start by checking in every morning and evening, and don't be sparing with praise or encouragement. You might want to make a particular effort to ensure that traditions you have fostered in person are brought online. Sharing recipes, launching virtual fitness classes and establishing social clubs are just some of the better ideas we've encountered.

Conflict Management

Conflict management refers to the extent that interpersonal tensions are managed for the greater good. No organisation can avoid conflict, particularly in conditions of heightened ambiguity. The only question is how quickly and effectively conflict gets resolved.

In our practice, over 90% of organisations are experiencing issues with conflict management when we start working together – some of them severe. Overly 'nice' cultures can be particularly toxic in this regard, as they can actively work to stop necessary conversations taking place.

Left unchecked, remote working can exacerbate conflict management issues. Communication can become inefficient; people feel as though they have limited healthy avenues to express their concerns; technology can become a counter productive substitute for effective communication. Fail to manage conflict amongst your remote workforce, and you will fail to create a resilient, responsive and innovation-focused working culture.

The first fix for remote working: call a team meeting to discuss how you're going to enable healthy conflict management. Discuss how to tackle the challenges that come from being physically separated – not least the fact that tone is easy to misconstrue in many forms of non-verbal communication. Consider creating a playbook, or at least some sort of code of conduct to which your team members all agree.

Connection

People working in resilient and innovation-focused cultures tend to have a high functioning sense of connectedness with others. Remote working can challenge this in novel ways – in particular, how available leaders expect their teams to be, and to what ends.

It is critical to ensure that you have the right online tooling to set your team up for success and make collaboration seamless. But it is also necessary to look into how you can strike a balance between work and family commitments.

But the concept of connection extends way beyond this. In Deep Work, the author Cal Newport describes the importance of being able to focus on tasks that require intense concentration in a distraction-free environment (another phrase for this is 'being in flow'.) Strategy, organisational design and ideation are all examples of 'deep work' tasks – and, in theory, ones that remote working is well placed to enable.

Yet, without active consideration and management, there is a danger that organisations simply create another form of presenteeism – one that disables their ability to do deep work, and creates greater inefficiency in the operating system.

The first fix for remote working: agree protocols for the use of your communication channels – and specifically the issue of when you expect your team members to be 'on' and 'off', and why.

If culture is the operating system of an organisation, the need to transition to remote working represents a significant update to the firmware. And with that update comes choices. The primary one is this: ignore the impact on your culture, and watch productivity suffer – or actively lean in, and transform how you work for good.

About Phil Lewis

After nearly 20 years in consulting, Phil Lewis founded Corporate Punk on the belief that there was a different and more effective way to drive change within organisations. He and his team help their clients transform their business performance by improving their resilience, responsiveness and innovation potential. Over the last five years, Corporate Punk has made a lasting impact on global businesses including Sony Music, the BBC and KPMG, as well as a range of PE and VC-backed high-growth firms.

In 2019, Phil was recognised as one of the UK's leading innovation consultants by the Management Consultancies Association. He also writes a column on leadership strategy for Forbes, which is syndicated around the world.

Prior to Corporate Punk, Phil's consulting experience included Adidas, ASOS, Zoopla, River Island, Thomas Cook and Hyundai. He also led strategy in some of the world's most highly regarded creative businesses.

Website: corporatepunk.com

Email: office@corporatepunk.com

LinkedIn: www.linkedin.com/in/philjlewis

Twitter: twitter.com/PhilLewisHQ

Why Working From Home Will Change Your Life

Ben Phillips

I'll admit it – the first time I sat down at my laptop at the kitchen table to work from home some years ago, it felt strange. I felt a mixture of emotions – pangs of guilt, a degree of excitement, pride in being *trusted enough* to work from home, and a similar sensation to that of being caught doing something naughty at school.

Those many years back, the number of companies agreeable to a percentage of their workforce being based at home was far less than today, but given changing global circumstances and a highly online-enabled workforce this is a situation many employees now find themselves in.

Reading this book, working from home or *working remotely* as the common description has now become (by implication – working away from your usual colleagues and workplace) you may be wondering how you can be most effective in your new home-bound environment. Can work and home ever co-exist with an effective mutual balance? What are you going to achieve? How do you avoid getting interrupted? Can you still be effectively managed and effectively manage others remotely?

To address some of these questions I will share with you three reasons why working from home will change your life.

1. Build Trust With Your Employer

"Trust" – a word which Customer Experience professionals like me use all the time; to describe the ideal status of a company-customer relationship. It's taken a while, but companies are now adopting the same principles of trusting their workforce to operate efficiently and deliver results whilst not operating under the traditional clock-in, clock-out working pattern.

There are, on occasion, stories of employees flouting that level of trust but on the whole I believe this is something which has matured over time, having become more widely accepted by employers whilst enabling employees to self-manage under these circumstances.

At the time of writing, recent global conditions have exposed some companies as not being very well set up for home working, where computer systems and databases cannot be accessed remotely or without a working Virtual Private Network (VPN). Clearly there will also be some employees who are also entirely unable to permit staff to work from home due to the nature of their professions; doctors, nurses, plumbers, builders, etc.

However, assuming working from home is possible in your walk of life, and that is the reason you have picked up this book, cementing that trust-based relationship with your employer will come down to a short-list of things:

- Can you responsibly self-manage your day to day activity?
- Can you benefit from a remote working set up to generate quality output?
- Are you able to still achieve your role objectives whilst working remotely?
- Are you still able to communicate effectively with your colleagues and customers?
- Can you find practical ways to deal with interruptions and discipline yourself to shut out the family, the dog and the doorbell?

On the last point above, I'm fortunate enough to have been working from home long enough to have set up my own home office – a dedicated workspace – no longer using the kitchen table or the sofa in the conservatory. Because of this I have become quite adept at compartmentalising my role duties whilst shutting out any chaos going on outside my office door (believe me, there can be a fair amount at any point in time in my house). So well have I been able to settle into this arrangement, we've moved house more than once over the years and the new office gets set up within a few hours and I'm ready to get underway with work once again.

Self-employed? You are your own boss? Then your situation is different, admittedly, but the principles above still apply, and in fact are borne out of the same best practices any self-employed person should adopt in order to drive their own objectives and ensure their enterprise is a success.

If you can abide by the above principles of what *good looks like* when working remotely, this may open up a better trust-based relationship with your employer so they are more agreeable to your need to work from home in the future.

2. Improve The Quality Of Your Work

Taking into account the fact that some employees *switch* into work mode when walking through the office door, leaving everything else outside to fully concentrate on the day job, how can you achieve the same levels of high quality work output when home-based?

Whilst the perception might be that you are most effective when working in your company environment, you might not actually be as effective as you think. Take an office-based role for example – think of how many times the phone rings whilst you are writing important emails; how many coffee breaks you take; the time queuing up at the sandwich shop at lunch time;

the endless meetings and a diary full of calls but no time to actually *do* the work; if you smoke, your accumulated cigarette breaks; the unintended interruptions because you can't put up a *Do Not Disturb* sign ... (whilst that would be nice).

Working from home almost immediately removes these barriers and frees up more quality time for you to be more effective. By *quality* time, I mean to do the following:

- Think creatively
- Concentrate on detailed tasks
- Plan with foresight
- Avoid avoidable mistakes
- Pause and reflect before submitting a project
- Proactively research, discover, explore new ideas
- Expand your knowledge
- Network with your peers
- Give back your time (e.g. charitable work)

... and then, more functionally:

- Clear out your inbox
- Check off specific task actions (satisfying!)
- Complete mandatory training
- Review and update your performance objectives

Of these two lists, we hardly ever get to do any of the top half and often leave what's in the bottom half until very late. Not that it's right, but for those of us who aren't black belts in time management, getting on top of all these activities can prove to be tough.

With better focus and the increased levels of concentration that may be possible at home you may be amazed at the improvement in the quality and timeliness of your work. I can honestly say that I have produced some of the best work of my career in the past few years I have been based at home, including high quality presentations, future-proofed planning and new thought leadership articles.

As well as finding the spare time to write and publish books ...

3. Establish A Better Work/Life Balance

One thing no home-based worker will ever tell you they miss is a long daily commute to and from a workplace. I did it myself years ago and resolved to never do so again – up and down the mainline train to London, standing together with folks coughing and sneezing their way into the day. Two hours later I'd arrive at work, exhausted before I'd even begun.

So, working from home you now have none of the associated costs nor the stress of commuting. And believe it or not, you'll notice how life goes on when you would have normally left the house. The kids head off to school, the postman delivers the mail, and, yes, the stock market continues to operate smoothly whether you are at home or not.

In the section above we talked about all the proactive and positive things you can do with more quality time. By replacing an hour or more of commuting with breakfast with the family, some much needed extra sleep or simply starting your working day sooner, this puts you in a far better position to get more from your working life.

Don't beat yourself up over how your day plays out, either. Work and life activities need to flex around each other when you're based at home, so don't watch the clock or feel guilty because you sat down at your laptop at 5 past the hour rather than on the hour. Where you lose out one day pick it back up again the next.

Your day is finally done? Achieved everything you wanted?

Or maybe not? The point is your life is but a few short steps away, not a car drive through the rain and traffic or a fight through crowds on the subway.

One thing my family picked up on after I started working from home regularly is how much more relaxed I had become. Put simply, I became a nicer bloke. When you consider all the many varied stresses, trials and tribulations of life, your job itself need not be one of those things.

Being set up well at home to conduct your role professionally, enjoy doing it and have the ability to separate work from life is the best recipe for personal success I can think of.

4. Bonus Section...It's About Your Bum

I couldn't resist ending my chapter without providing you with one final piece of advice:

Invest in a good chair!

Depending on your age and how keen your father was on imparting his sage knowledge, you may have been advised at some point to invest in a pair of good shoes. Why? Because you have to walk in them every day.

Your designated working from home chair is just the same. You and that chair are going to become seriously well acquainted as you settle into your new environment, and the kitchen bar stool, deck chair from the garden or low-sofa just won't cut it anymore. So do your bum a favour – invest wisely.

About Ben Phillips

Ben Phillips CCXP has a 15 year career in Customer Experience having worked with some of the world's top market research firms, technology companies and consultancies.

Ben is a #1 author, having contributed to *Customer Experience* published by Writing Matters in Dec 2019. In between global travel for his role as Head of CX with Nielsen, he spends time with his family, plays jazz bass guitar, supports Tottenham Hotspur and drinks real ales.

LinkedIn: linkedin.com/in/ben-phillips-ccxp

Thank You

At the time of writing the world is literally in lockdown due to the coronavirus pandemic (Covid-19). This means millions of people are now required to work from home.

For many nothing changed, but for too many this has been a total culture shock.

This book was written and published in one week because we saw a massive need - on a global scale - to get something of high value into the hands of professionals who need help now - not in three months time.

Publishing an outstanding book is not possible under normal conditions - but these are not normal conditions.

So firstly, to the authors, thanks for giving your very best cut-through advice.

Secondly, thanks to the great people at Thomas Power Club (TPC) and especially Michelle D Harris who has the remarkable skill of being able to get the best out a diverse group of high end professionals.

And lastly, thank you - the reader - for buying the book.

We are confident this book will provide invaluable practical help and generous encouragement and moral support.

Printed in Poland
by Amazon Fulfillment
Poland Sp. z o.o., Wrocław

58268151R00115